RUSSIAN MILITARY

GROUND FORCE MODERNIZATION AND GEORGIA WAR LESSONS

DEFENSE, SECURITY AND STRATEGIES

Additional books in this series can be found on Nova's website
under the Series tab.

Additional E-books in this series can be found on Nova's website
under the E-book tab.

RUSSIAN POLITICAL, ECONOMIC AND SECURITY ISSUES

Additional books in this series can be found on Nova's website
under the Series tab.

Additional E-books in this series can be found on Nova's website
under the E-book tab.

DEFENSE, SECURITY AND STRATEGIES

RUSSIAN MILITARY

GROUND FORCE MODERNIZATION AND GEORGIA WAR LESSONS

Alessandra R. Guardano

EDITOR

Nova Science Publishers, Inc.
New York

For permission to use material from this book please contact us:
Telephone 631-231-7269; Fax 631-231-8175
Web Site: http://www.novapublishers.com

NOTICE TO THE READER

The Publisher has taken reasonable care in the preparation of this book, but makes no expressed or implied warranty of any kind and assumes no responsibility for any errors or omissions. No liability is assumed for incidental or consequential damages in connection with or arising out of information contained in this book. The Publisher shall not be liable for any special, consequential, or exemplary damages resulting, in whole or in part, from the readers' use of, or reliance upon, this material. Any parts of this book based on government reports are so indicated and copyright is claimed for those parts to the extent applicable to compilations of such works.

Independent verification should be sought for any data, advice or recommendations contained in this book. In addition, no responsibility is assumed by the publisher for any injury and/or damage to persons or property arising from any methods, products, instructions, ideas or otherwise contained in this publication.

This publication is designed to provide accurate and authoritative information with regard to the subject matter covered herein. It is sold with the clear understanding that the Publisher is not engaged in rendering legal or any other professional services. If legal or any other expert assistance is required, the services of a competent person should be sought. FROM A DECLARATION OF PARTICIPANTS JOINTLY ADOPTED BY A COMMITTEE OF THE AMERICAN BAR ASSOCIATION AND A COMMITTEE OF PUBLISHERS.

Additional color graphics may be available in the e-book version of this book.

Library of Congress Cataloging-in-Publication Data

Russian military : ground force modernization and Georgia war lessons / editor, Alessandra R. Guardano.
    p. cm.
  Includes index.
  ISBN 978-1-62100-347-2 (hbk.)
  1. South Ossetia War, 2008. 2. Russia (Federation). Russkaia Armiia.--History--21st century. 3. Russia (Federation). Russkaia Armiia.--Organization. 4. Russia (Federation)--Military policy. I. Guardano, Alessandra R. II. Thornton, Rod. III. Hamilton, Robert E. Russian military and the Georgia war. IV. Cohen, Ariel. Russian military and the Georgia war. V. Army War College (U.S.). Strategic Studies Institute. VI. Title: Ground force modernization and Georgia war lessons.
  DK679.S68R87 2011
  355.30947--dc23
                2011033362

Published by Nova Science Publishers, Inc. † New York

CONTENTS

PREFACE

Russia launched the war against Georgia in August 2008 for highly valued strategic and geopolitical objectives, which included de facto annexation of Abkhazia, weakening or toppling the Mikheil Saakashvili regime, and preventing the North Atlantic Treaty Organization (NATO) enlargement. This book examines the Georgian war along with the recent process of organizational change in the Russian ground forces.

Chapter 1- This monograph examines the recent process of organizational change in the Russian ground forces. It begins by charting the whole post-Soviet military reform debate. This debate was dominated, on the one hand, by those seeking to make the armed forces more professional, flexible, and adroit—and thus better suited to the security demands of a major 21st-century power—and, on the other hand, by senior military figures wedded to the concepts of mass and a conscript- based military. It was actually only after the war with Georgia in 2008, and when military opposition was weakened, that change within the ground forces could begin in earnest. New command tiers were established, divisions became brigades, and the idea of absorbing professional soldiers into the ground forces was refined. The problems of generating a suitable corps of non-commissioned officers, of training suit-able officers, and of marrying equipment to strategic need are all issues covered here. This work concludes with the thought that even though the changes being introduced in the ground forces look dramatic, they cannot be implemented overnight. The road towards fundamental change where Russia's ground forces are concerned will be quite a long one.

Chapter 2- Russia launched the war against Georgia in August 2008 for highly valued strategic and geopolitical objectives, which included de facto annexation of Abkhazia, weakening or toppling the Mikheil Saakashvili regime, and preventing North Atlantic Treaty Organization (NATO) enlargement. The Russian politico-military elites had focused on Georgia since the days of the presidency of Eduard Shevardnadze, whom they blamed, together with Soviet president Mikhail Gorbachev and Union of Socialist Soviet Republics (USSR) Communist Party Central Committee Secretary Alexander Yakovlev, for the dissolution of the Soviet empire in Eastern Europe and the dismantlement of the Soviet Union itself.[1]

Russian post-communist security establishments also viewed the attractive Abkhaz coast line and illicit business opportunities provided by lawless Abkhazia and South Ossetia as additional incentives for deep involvement along the metropolitan periphery. Russian military

---

[1] Ronald D. Asmus, *A Little War That Shook the World*, New York: Palgrave-MacMillan, 2010, p. viii.

and covert action support of secessionist movements there starting in 1992 should be seen along this continuum. Things only got worse after pro-American, NATO, and European Union (EU) oriented Mikheil Saakashvili was elected president. Since 2006, the military operation rapidly became the matter of "when," not if.

In: Russian Military: Ground Force Modernization...   ISBN: 978-1-62100-347-2
Editor: Alessandra R. Guardano   © 2012 Nova Science Publishers, Inc.

Chapter 1

MILITARY MODERNIZATION AND THE RUSSIAN GROUND FORCES[*]

Rod Thornton

The Strategic Studies Institute (SSI) is part of the U.S. Army War College and is the strategic-level study agent for issues related to national security and military strategy with emphasis on geostrategic analysis.

The mission of SSI is to use independent analysis to conduct strategic studies that develop policy recommendations on:

- Strategy, planning, and policy for joint and combined employment of military forces;
- Regional strategic appraisals;
- The nature of land warfare;
- Matters affecting the Army's future;
- The concepts, philosophy, and theory of strategy; and
- Other issues of importance to the leadership of the Army.

Studies produced by civilian and military analysts concern topics having strategic implications for the Army, the Department of Defense, and the larger national security community.

In addition to its studies, SSI publishes special reports on topics of special or immediate interest. These include edited proceedings of conferences and topically-oriented roundtables, expanded trip reports, and quick-reaction responses to senior Army leaders.

The Institute provides a valuable analytical capability within the Army to address strategic and other issues in support of Army participation in national security policy formulation.

---

[*] This is an edited, reformatted and augmented version of a Strategic Studies Institute publication.

SSI Monograph

The views expressed in this report are those of the author and do not necessarily reflect the official policy or position of the Department of the Army, the Department of Defense, or the U.S. Government. Authors of Strategic Studies Institute (SSI) publications enjoy full academic freedom, provided they do not disclose classified information, jeopardize operations security, or misrepresent official U.S. policy. Such academic freedom empowers them to offer new and sometimes controversial perspectives in the interest of furthering debate on key issues.

*****

This publication is subject to Title 17, United States Code, Sections 101 and 105. It is in the public domain and may not be copyrighted.

Foreword

Military organizations have to change with the times. But organizations, of course, resist change; military organizations resist change more than most; and, it can be argued, Russian military organizations resist change more than most military organizations. This is clear from the pace of the post-Cold War attempts to reform the Russian ground forces.

Historically, this was an army that, in many ways, sacrificed the need for military efficiency in order to perform a role as the inculcator of Soviet values into young conscripts. Social engineering then mattered almost more than military skill. But today, in the era of high-tech weaponry and expeditionary warfare, armies all across the world can no longer remain simply as 2-year repositories for unmotivated conscript soldiers. Thus it has long been recognized in Moscow's political circles that the "citizen-army" must be replaced by modern, flexible, and well-trained ground forces. The Russian leadership believes that such forces would better protect the country and serve the government as an adjunct to its foreign and security policy.

Indeed, it is the likes of President Vladimir Putin and Prime Minister Dimitry Medvedev who have been the main instigators of reform—wanting their armed forces to be more capable operationally. The politicians have been facing the resistance of conservative gener- als, and for several years there has been stalemate in the reform process. However, the war with Georgia in 2008 showed the overall weaknesses of the Russian military, and thus undermined the opposition of the generals. Significant change could now come. The Russian ground forces are therefore now undergoing quite significant reform in terms of structure, deploy- ability, and overall philosophy. U.S. military planners must be mindful that, if all that is anticipated comes to pass, these Russian ground forces are now set to shake off many of their old Soviet failings and deficiencies.

DOUGLAS C. LOVELACE, JR. Director
Strategic Studies Institute

ABOUT THE AUTHOR

ROD THORNTON lectures at the University of Nottingham in the United Kingdom (UK). He previously spent 9 years in a British Army infantry regiment, including 3 years in Northern Ireland and 1 year as a Serbo-Croat interpreter in Bosnia (1992-93). He has lived and worked in both Moscow and Sarajevo. Dr. Thornton taught for 5 years at the UK's Joint Services Command and Staff College (working for King's College London), which included guest lecturing at the NATO Defense College in Rome, Italy. Dr. Thornton is the author of *Asymmetric Warfare: Threat and Response in the 21st Century* (2007) and is currently working on a book (with Dr. Bettina Renz) on Russian military modernization. Dr. Thornton holds a Ph.D. in comparative peacekeeping operations.

SUMMARY

This monograph examines the recent process of organizational change in the Russian ground forces. It begins by charting the whole post-Soviet military reform debate. This debate was dominated, on the one hand, by those seeking to make the armed forces more professional, flexible, and adroit—and thus better suited to the security demands of a major 21st-century power—and, on the other hand, by senior military figures wedded to the concepts of mass and a conscript- based military. It was actually only after the war with Georgia in 2008, and when military opposition was weakened, that change within the ground forces could begin in earnest. New command tiers were established, divisions became brigades, and the idea of absorbing professional soldiers into the ground forces was refined. The problems of generating a suitable corps of non-commissioned officers, of training suitable officers, and of marrying equipment to strategic need are all issues covered here. This work concludes with the thought that even though the changes being introduced in the ground forces look dramatic, they cannot be implemented overnight. The road towards fundamental change where Russia's ground forces are concerned will be quite a long one.

INTRODUCTION

Change is not a common commodity in Russia. The country, whether as Tsarist Russia, the Soviet Union, or as today's democratic manifestation, is not one characterized by entrepreneurship, drive, and innovation. Rather, as any historian of this land would aver, it is one beset by torpor, indolence, and conservatism. So the current ambition of the political leadership in Russia to push through a state-wide process of *modernizatsiya* (modernization) is bound to be one that, to a large degree, must fall on deaf ears. And while the main target of this process is obviously the economy, the Russian military has also been asked to undertake considerable reform.

For the political leaders involved in trying to push through such reform, the task has naturally not been easy. The military hierarchy in Russia, itself imbued with considerable institutional power, has been doing its best to stand against change; against those reforms that threaten not just the comfort of familiar strategies, structures, and standard operating procedures, but also the individual stakes of senior officers within the various military organizations. Ultimately, the proposed reforms threaten the very jobs of such officers. The Russian military, as a whole, does not want to modernize; or rather it does not want *to be "modernized"* in the way that its political masters want.

The aim here is to analyze this current process of Russian military modernization. More specifically, this work is concerned with examining modernization in the Russian army; and particularly in the ground forces. While making occasional comments about the airborne forces, this is an arm of service separate from the ground forces. In this monograph, the term "army" will be used to include both airborne and ground forces. As a point of detail, the Russian word *armiya* is often mistranslated as "army," when it actually means *all* of the country's armed forces, i.e., the range of armed services controlled by the Ministry of Defense (MoD)—including the navy and the air force. This causes some confusion for Western analysts, particularly in trying to establish the actual manpower figures that relate to the *armiya*. Such an issue is compounded by the tendency of Russian observers and analysts to be somewhat inaccurate with their use of figures.

Such caveats having been established, the following analysis will focus on the process of military modernization in terms of its manifestation in structural and personnel terms in regard to the Russian ground forces. While some mention will be made of equipment issues and technical advances, these are not so important; mostly because there have been very few such advances made.

Mention will first be made of the background to the current wave of Russian military modernization. This will be followed by a look at the role of the 2008 war with Georgia in terms of giving impetus to a reform process that had been stalling. The new structure of the ground forces will then be examined, followed by a look at the changes made in terms of personnel issues. By way of conclusion, some broad comments will be made in regard to the current efficacy of Russia's ground forces.

HISTORY OF POST-SOVIET MILITARY REFORM

The last Soviet leader, Mikhail Gorbachev, first set in motion the process of military reform that the ending of the Cold War so demanded. He looked upon his military machine as a gargantuan, inflexible dinosaur that absorbed immense state resources, while seemingly providing for very little in the way of operational utility in the defense and security realm—at least compared to the U.S. armed forces. Despite his wishes, all that Gorbachev could push through in terms of change was to bring down the overall personnel strength of the armed forces from five to four million.

Boris Yeltsin, the first president of the newly constituted Russia, kept up the pressure on the military to reform. Yeltsin wanted cutbacks. In particular, he wanted to see the end of Russia's conscript military to be replaced by a much smaller, professional one—akin to those in the United States and the United Kingdom (UK). The principal political goals in terms of ending conscription, however, were not so much to develop a more efficient military—although that would have been a welcome side-effect—rather, Yeltsin wanted to both save money and to court electoral popularity.

In terms of cost savings, Yeltsin and his government of economic technocrats wanted to see an end to the conscription system that was a drain on the economy in that it took young men out of the work force for the 2 years of their service. Conscription was also tied to another generator of vast expense: the mobilization system. Reducing the former would also reduce the need for the latter. The mobilization system was one wherein, in times of crisis or outright conflict, a huge number of former conscripts—up to 20 million—could be called up. This, though, meant maintaining a large number of bases manned only by a cadre staff—including many officers—whose sole task it was to keep the base and its associated equipment (tanks, armored personnel carriers [APCs], etc.) prepared for any possible influx of mobilized former conscripts—an influx, of course, that might never happen. Moreover, to add to the cost of the mobilization system much of Russian industry had to maintain the capacity to reengineer both plant and human skills to turn out supporting materiel for this 20 million-man military. This was naturally an inefficient use of resources. The new idea was to replace the conscript military with a professional one. Recruits would sign 3-year contracts. This, naturally, would mean a smaller military. It would thus require fewer bases, less infrastructure, and fewer officers to run it. It would also not generate a mass of conscripts, and thus the mobilization system would have to be either drastically reduced or actually eliminated. The ending, therefore, of both conscription and the associated mobilization system offered the chance to make huge financial savings. This was very tempting to a Russian government that was, in the early 1990s, looking to cut costs wherever it could.

The cost effectiveness of a smaller military would also be enhanced by the fact that it would be more efficient, more flexible, and, crucially in this immediate post-Cold War era, more deployable and thus of more use as an adjunct to Russia's striving to play a significant role in world affairs. The argument was also being made that professional service personnel— the contractees (*kontraktniki* in Russian) would have a greater chance of developing the skills necessary to handle the increasingly complicated military technologies that were by now coming into service.

A further reason for Yeltsin wanting to see an end to conscription was that it would prove popular at the ballot box. Most Russians looked upon conscription as an iniquitous and hateful institution. Few young men wanted to join a military in which hazing was rife, housing poor, and treatment bad. The electorate would support any politician who called for conscription's termination.

Naturally enough, though, there was opposition from within the military to Yeltsin's proposed reforms. An end to both the conscription and mobilization systems, and the moves towards a smaller professional military, would patently mean that thousands of officers' jobs would be lost; mostly in the cadre formations. And, of course, among those losing their jobs in all this shake-up would be a good many generals. And these generals, often within the bloated General Staff (where some 21,000 officers worked), could generate a fair degree of political clout since they constituted one of the principal *siloviki* (power) structures in Russia. The generals could stand in opposition to the proposed reforms; and, of course, they did.

The first point made by many a senior Russian military officer, both serving and retired, was that the country needed conscription because it served a useful role in shaping Russian society. The military, indeed, saw itself as a force for social good. There was a sense that all young Russian men should experience conscript service as a means of creating a sense of national pride. Previously, in Soviet times, the military had been the only state institution that could develop in young men, from Lithuania to Kyrgyzstan, and from Novaya Zemlya to

Sakhalin, a sense of "sovietness," of nationhood. This same principal still applied, said many a post-Soviet general, in the new Russia. Who was to instill the sense of Russian national spirit if not the military? It was, after all, the only institution to which virtually all young Russian men would at one time belong.[1]

The point was also made that conscript service was a "right of passage": that the young Russian male owed an immense debt of gratitude to the state that had nurtured him. He then should pay that debt off by serving in the military. As the current Deputy Chief of the General Staff, and himself an arch conservative, Colonel-General Vasiliy Smirnov,[2] put it, conscription was necessary because "every citizen should be ready to defend the state."[3] Everyone, he went on, had to be "taught to respect their constitutional duty to defend the country."[4]

Of course, all such sentiments really belonged in the bygone Soviet era. But the mindsets of those in the Russian military who had by then (early-to-mid1990s) reached one-star rank and above were forged in this former Soviet era—and their thinking died hard.

On a more prosaic level, the argument could also be made that the Russian military was different from Western militaries in that they did not have to face the possibility of conflict with China. Russia sees China, short as it is of the raw materials necessary to maintain its economic growth, as being covetous of Siberia's wealth of natural resources. In any possible future military enagagement between the two countries, the Chinese would doubtless field a mass army of conscripts. So, of course, say many a Russian general, Russia has to do likewise. The ability, then, to mobilize a huge number of former conscripts would clearly be needed as part of Russia's defense against this perceived Chinese threat.

Most of all, though, the generals' opposition to the ending of the conscript system was a matter of supreme self-interest. Conscripts, when hired out by officers as cheap labor to local enterprises or farms, provide a means for many an officer to supplement what are fairly meager salaries. Such schemes produce profits for officers all the way up the chain of command. The corrupt practices engaged in by a good proportion of the military's senior ranks do not stop there: a decent number were and are involved in siphoning off funds meant for weapons procurement and construction projects into their private businesses or bank accounts. Being a Russian general is, in many cases, a ticket to some riches.

However, senior officers also pointed out the human cost of markedly reducing the size of the military and thus the number of officers within it. Severe hardships could result. For if officers lost their jobs, then they and their families would also lose their homes— and this in a country already critically short of housing. Of course, the jobs that the generals most feared losing were their own. A conscript army meant a large army, and thus many generals would be needed to run it. A reformed, professional army would be smaller and need fewer officers and thus fewer generals. Any senior officer who backed the reforms demanded by Yeltsin and his government would be akin to a turkey voting for Christmas.

Undaunted, however, by such military conservatism, Yeltsin issued an edict in 1996 instructing the entire military to begin a process of "professionalization." By the end of 2000, it was stated, all Russian military personnel would be on contracts. Conscription would then have ended.[5]

In choosing which formations would be the first to be professionalized, the main criterion was to select those that would most likely be engaged on operations. The idea was that it would only be the formations manned by professionals who would conduct any fighting that needed to be done by Russian forces— notably in Chechnya. Yeltsin wanted to avoid having conscripts involved—and dying—in combat. Again, it lost votes. The first formation chosen to become fully manned by *kontraktniki* was the 76th Airborne Division (as it was then called) in Pskov.[6] The scheme was later to take in other formations in the airborne forces and those engaged on operations—i.e., the 42nd Motor Rifle Division (MRD), then involved in combat in Chechnya.

Having been given targets to introduce *kontraktniki* into such formations, some skullduggery was entered into by senior officers to massage the recruitment figures to their advantage. The more it *seemed* as if the professionalization process was going well, then the less pressure would be put on the military by its political masters. Since, for instance, not many of the new *kontraktniki* wanted to sign up to serve in the 42nd MRD, and thus to commit to 3 years spent solely in Chechnya, certain "transfers" went ahead. When elements of the 76th were about to leave Chechnya after a short deployment there, 1,000 of its *kontraktniki* were, apparently, simply transferred over to the 42nd. They were thus counted twice: once as part of the 76th and then again as troops of the 42nd. On paper, it seemed as if both formations had achieved their targets for *kontraktniki* recruitment.[7] Another scam was to force conscripts to sign on as *kontraktniki*. They would then be paid as professionals but actually leave when their 2-year conscript term was up, and not when their 3-year contract term finished. Such servicemen were not committed to a military career and thus had no intention of signing on for further periods of contract service. Again, it seemed as if there were more truly *kontraktniki* than was actually the case.[8] With all such hoodwinking, the generals could tell their political masters that the scheme to professionalize the military was progressing well, therefore those masters would not press them to recruit more *kontraktniki* —which they wanted to avoid. The military had to remain conscript.

Other schemes to undermine the professionalization process were also entered into. Projects to build new barracks and housing for single and married *kontraktniki* went either painfully slowly or were simply not completed due to foot-dragging by the General Staff. The bills presented by the military for such projects were too high, making it seem as if professionalization could not be afforded. Moreover, the *kontraktniki* who had been promised decent living conditions, only to find out that they did not yet exist, would not be signing on for a further 3 years once their initial term was up. Pay was another issue. The *kontraktniki* could not be paid more than quite senior officers. And since the latter's pay was so low, the *kontraktniki* themselves had to accept low salaries. Promises to raise pay scales were not kept. There was thus little financial incentive to become a professional soldier. *Kontraktniki* recruitment, quite strong to begin with in the late 1990s, began to trail off as the situation became clearer in regard to both accommodation and pay.[9]

While the mission to create a professional military seemed destined to remain a work in progress, Yeltsin did have some concrete successes where his efforts to reform the armed services were concerned. He had inherited a military some four million strong; but by 1992 this figure had dropped to 2.8 million, and it continued to fall further throughout the later 1990s.[10] This was not so much to do with any active attempts to reduce the size of the military, but rather came about both because of the increase in the number of post- Soviet deferments available to potential conscripts and because the pool of manpower that Russia now had access to was much smaller than that in the Soviet Union. What curiously did not change, though, and this was to the conservative generals' advantage, was the number of actual formations within the army's ground forces. This stayed the same—at 203 divisions.

In the later Soviet period, these 203 divisions were never all fully manned. Only 50 Category A divisions were described as being at "permanent readiness." The rest, the B, C, and D category formations, were cadre units; understrength and waiting to be filled out only on mobilization. The division's category depended on its manning strength and equipment schedules. A Category C division would, for instance, have a personnel strength of approximately 1,000—mainly officers and warrant officers.[11] In the post-Cold War era, the situation in terms of these divisions' manning levels became considerably "worse." Only some 13 percent of the ground forces' overall assets were now deemed ready to take part in immediate operations (i.e., without mobilization).

But while all these divisions were lacking in conscripts, what they did not lack was officers. These were still there acting in their role as the divisions' cadre strength. Thus there were divisions with only 1,000 or so personnel; half of whom would be officers or warrant officers. This was the obvious result of putting the fox in charge of the chicken coop. For here was a ruse by the military hierarchy to preserve officer posts: units needed officers—including generals—and so the units were kept.[12]

PUTIN ADVANCES REFORMS

Vladimir Putin, when he officially succeeded Yeltsin as president in 2000, picked up the baton of military reform. But whereas Yeltsin was concerned mostly with cost savings, Putin had a much more nationalist agenda and specifically wanted armed forces, and especially units of the airborne and ground forces, that could contribute to Russia's great power ambitions. The military Putin inherited, though, while it appeared to be large on paper, was actually a largely ineffectual fighting force and certainly not capable of deploying, with any appreciable size, on any expeditionary operation. Putin lamented that, "The army [i.e., the *armiya*] has 1.4 million men, but there is no one to wage war."[13]

Putin in particular directed his ire at the mobilization concept and at the hollow shell of a military that it had created. The thinking behind the mobilization concept had always been that the Soviet military would only ever be engaged in full-blown superpower conflict, and never in any small-scale, low-intensity engagements. The Soviet Union never conducted the likes of the operations that the U.S. military had done in such countries as Lebanon, the Dominican Republic, Grenada, and Panama; or as the British had done in the Falklands/Malvinas.

For the Soviet military, with its "big war" emphasis, the thinking was that any lead-up to such a war would involve a prior buildup of tension that would allow time for the mobilization of reservists. Hence there was no need for the Soviet military, apart obviously from formations based in East Germany, to be in any real state of readiness. The results of this approach were obvious during the Soviet army's war in Afghanistan in the 1980s. The battalions sent there (infantry, airborne, artillery, air defence, and logistics) were all composite and made up from manpower of the three undermanned battalions in any Soviet regiment. There was no sense that an entire regiment, let alone a division, would be available to be sent en bloc to Afghanistan.[14] This neglect of the concept of "rapid deployment" was still apparent when the Soviet military became (for the most part) that of Russia in 1991. Indeed, the battalions sent to fight in Chechnya were also composite in nature.[15]

But Putin wanted a military that did not have to wait for recalled conscripts to turn up or for composite units to be formed before it was ready either to defend the country or to deploy anywhere. In essence, what Putin wanted was the professional military that had still, by 2000 and in spite of Yeltsin's earlier edict, not yet materialized.

The problem remained the institutional power of the military. If the conservative generals wanted to thwart Putin's plans for military reform they could, just as they had done with Yeltsin. And Putin knew he had to treat them warily. As Aleksandr Golts puts it, Putin "didn't dare initiate radical military reform." Putin's power base lay with the domestic security service (the FSB)[16] and not with the FSB's rivals for institutional power, the military. But Putin did, though, think he could push through something like the Israeli system in which a professional force was always on hand that could, in slow times, be reinforced by recalled conscripts.

A good deal of military procrastination ensued. Several defensive measures were enacted to hinder this latest, Putin inspired, drive towards professionalization. The first card played by the conservative generals, led again by Colonel-General Smirnov, was that of cost. It was said that Russia could not afford the number of *kontraktniki* being proposed. The figures to back up the claims presented by the conservative elements within the powerful General Staff varied. In December 2001, the cost of professionalizing one division was stated as being 500 million roubles. By March 2002 the cost had risen to 1 billion roubles per division, and by May of that year it was 2.5 billion! So Putin then advanced the concept of just professionalizing several units and formations—such as those in the airborne forces and marines. These units would then be capable of deploying immediately without waiting for any recalled conscripts.[17] Thus, in 2003, Putin pushed through the Federal Targeted Program for the Conversion of the Military to Contract Service. Under this program, the number of *kontraktniki* was supposed to increase from 22,000 in 2003 to 148,000 by 2008.[18] In step with this move and echoing Yeltsin's desire to court public popularity by ending conscription, the principal 2-year conscript term of service was to be reduced; first to 18 months and then, in 2007, to just 1 year. The next step planned was that of the total abolition of conscription.[19]

But even this move was not to the liking of Smirnov and his allies. They continually revised downwards the target figure for the number of *kontraktniki*. The original figure of 148,000 *kontraktniki* posts to be created by 2008 was first dropped by the General Staff to 133,000, and then to 125,000. Finally, in January 2008, Smirnov announced that the overall program had been successfully completed, but with just 100,000 *kontraktniki*![20]

With such sabotaging of his wishes, Putin realized he needed help in pushing through his ideas on military reform. Thus in February 2007, he drafted in a new defense minister, Anatoliy Serdyukov. Here was the first truly civilian Russian minister of defense. As the former head of the Tax Ministry, Serdyukov was supposed to have a wealth of experience of dealing with bureaucracies and a nose for the corrupt practices in which many senior officers were engaging. This was a weakness that could be targeted. The more generals that could be caught and sacked for abusing their position, then the more of them that could be replaced by officers compliant to their political masters. Serdyukov thus conducted "a thorough purge" of the MoD.[21] To aid him in his mission, Serdyukov brought in a phalanx of advisers and bureaucrats from St. Petersburg — outsiders with no links to the Moscow military gravy train.[22]

While Serdyukov, like his predecessors, was capable of reducing the overall numbers in the military, the actual number of officers— particularly generals— was staying remarkably static. Serdyukov was also to point out an old issue. Even though the personnel strength of the military had dropped to just 1.3 million, the actual number of units and formations in the ground forces remained remarkably the same. Moreover, as Serdyukov noted, the officers serving in this skeleton army were all the time losing their leadership and administrative capabilities because they had no actual soldiers to lead or to administer. Certainly, it was fairly pointless for them to do any training or exercises. This system, said Serdyukov, meant that while the ground forces had its 203 divisions, it could only muster 90,000 combat-effective troops.[23] At least this was better than the figure quoted earlier by Putin in 2006 of only 55,000 combat-effective troops.[24] While representing something of an improvement, it was still clear that something was very wrong with the Russian army.

Thus it became Serdyukov's principal aim to reduce the entire military's officer strength by 200,000. He wanted to see officers constituting only some 15 percent of the total military strength, and not the 30 or so percent that they did constitute.[25] Basically, Serdyukov's plan ran like this: the 355,300 officers and 140,000 warrant officers reportedly on strength as of January 1, 2008 would be reduced, by January 1, 2012, to just 150,000 officers. All of the 140,000 warrant officers would lose their jobs (the rank would disappear). However, the number of other ranks was to be boosted from 623,500 to 850,000; 180,000 of whom were slated to be *kontraktniki* (both figures relate to the armed forces as a whole).[26] What Serdyukov was doing, and very much what he had in mind, was to eliminate the inverted rank pyramid that had formed. Thus while the jobs of many officers would be lost, the actual number of lieutenants in the armed forces was to rise by 10,000. The ultimate aim was to have, across the services, 10,000 officers of colonel rank and above; 40,000 lieutenant-colonels and majors and, at the base of the new pyramid, 100,000 junior officers (40,000 captains and 60,000 lieutenants).[27]

Serdyukov naturally clashed with the conservative Chief of the General Staff (CGS), General Yuriy Baluyevsky, whose attempts to thwart Serdyukov eventually led to his replacement as CGS in June 2008 by General Nikolai Makarov. Makarov would doubtless prove to be more receptive to politically-driven reform than his predecessor. Unlike Baluyevsky, Makarov had no power base in Moscow among the General Staff—he had been brought in from his previous post as the head of the Siberian Military District. As such, he owed his position to the political masters who had appointed him, and not to his standing among the generals of Moscow's General Staff. He would thus more likely be a proponent of what those political masters wanted, i.e., reform. Of course, the more Makarov supported the politicians' reform processes, the more enemies he would make in the General Staff and the more he would then have to rely on political patronage to keep him in his post as CGS. For Putin and Serdyukov, it was a virtuous circle. Makarov was just a puppet to be manipulated by them.

Despite now having a defense minister and a CGS who were minded to push through reform—which came to be called the process of *modernizatsiya* — the conservative elements in the military were still capable of at least delaying, if not exactly thwarting, the process. This all changed, however, after the war with Georgia broke out in August 2008.

THE WAR WITH GEORGIA

While perceived in some quarters as a war that Russia was well prepared for and one that was perhaps even instigated by Moscow, this was actually not the case. The Russian armed forces were just not ready to fight: the initiation of the conflict took both politicians and military by surprise. The response to the Georgian attack on South Ossetia—and on the Russian peacekeeping troops there—was slow. This was partly due to the fact that neither civilian nor military decisionmakers were available in the August holiday period. As the newspaper, *Moskovskiy Komsomolets*, reported, "They could not find the defense minister via telephone for more than 10 hours" and "could not make any important decisions without him."[28] Confusion was also apparent over whether the despatch of troops should be authorized by Prime Minister Putin or by President Medvedev. Technically, such power lay with the president, but Putin was still looked upon as the major locus of power within the government. More critically for detailed military activity, Colonel-General Aleksandr Rukshin, the head of the Defense Ministry's Main Operations Directorate (the department responsible for planning operations beyond Russia's borders and the "brain of the General Staff"[29]), had not been replaced since his removal by Serdyukov back in July. Indeed, most of the officers in the Directorate were away on leave, and the Directorate's building was itself being redecorated. No one was there. Rukshin apparently even refused an appeal from the Defense Ministry to return to duty to cover the crisis. It was only a call from Putin that actually brought him back to his desk.

The problems at the Directorate may have slowed down response times, but there was little excuse for the slow reaction of elements of the ground forces' 58th Army. The 135th and 693rd Motor Rifle Regiments of the 19th Division were based just over the border from South Ossetia and yet were so slow to come to action that troops from the airborne forces, flying in from hundreds of kilometers away and acting as basic infantry, still managed to be the first Russian combat forces to cross the border into South Ossetia itself.[30]

Apart from the organizational *faux pas*, the war also exposed other Russian military inadequacies. Firstly, space-based and electronic warfare (EW) assets failed to pick up the concentration of Georgian forces prior to the conflict. And neither could Russian EW suppress the Georgians' air defense capabilities (leading to the shooting down of several Russian aircraft). Reconnaissance assets were also rudimentary and provided little in the way of information to turn into actionable intelligence.[31]

Poor communications in theatre added to other command and control problems. Interservice cooperation was minimal, particularly air-to-ground. The commander of the North Caucasus Military District seemingly had no control of what the air force was doing in his theater of operations. Air assets were controlled by the Air Force commander, Colonel-General Aleksandr Zelin, who remained remote from the battlefield. The retired general and author, Makhmut Gareyev, noted that the "absence of a unified command" was the root cause of Russian aircraft losses and of the failure of the air force to provide effective close air support to ground units.[32] Basic tactical communications were also woeful. Apparently, even the commander of the 58th Army, Lieutenant-General Anatoliy Khrulev, at one point could only communicate with some of his troops via a satellite phone he had borrowed from a journalist.[33]

The Russian equivalent of the Global Positioning System (*Global"naya Navigatsionayya Sputnikovaya Sistema* [GLONASS]) did not work properly. In 1996 there were 21 satellites in the GLONASS array, but by the beginning of 1998 only 16 were still transmitting. This first generation of Russian satellites was poor, and no enhanced replacements were initially deployed due to budgetary cutbacks. Six more satellites were launched between 1998 and 2000, these could not compensate for the fall-out rate of the older satellites, and by 2001 there were only seven still operating. This situation had not improved much by 2008 when the war with Georgia began.[34]

The failings of GLONASS not only affected basic navigational tasks and fire control missions, but also made it impossible to fashion a network-centric capability (NCC). Thus, overall command and control was inept at best. Luckily, individual units did what they had to do and initiative was displayed, especially by the airborne units involved.[35] The war was saved for Russia by what Medvedev called the "professional, independent operations of battalions."[36]

The lack of basic modern equipment was evident elsewhere. Russian tanks, besides lacking access to GLONASS, were also without identification friendor-foe (IFF) systems and thermal imagers. The tanks themselves were principally (60-75 percent) older T- 62s or T-72s, which had no answer to the Georgians' use of shaped-charge warheads. Artillery units did not have counterbattery radar and so could not locate Georgian fire bases. All troops, bar some special forces units, lacked night-vision aids, and their armored vests were heavy and cumbersome. All in all, not much was in the Russians' favor, and yet they proved victorious. As one Russian journalist put it, "It's just that we had a bit less chaos than the Georgians."[37]

In terms of Russian personnel involved in this war, those units that had a fair number of *kontraktniki* within their ranks were perceived to have performed better than those that did not. A lack of leadership skills was also apparent; especially at the noncomissioned officer (NCO) level. For instance, basic issues such as the filling of tanks' reactive-armor canisters prior to operations — an NCO task in any Western army—could not be performed because it required the presence of an officer of at least captain rank. But these were all too busy on other tasks. Thus ground forces tanks went into battle with empty reactive-armor canisters.[38]

Naturally, once the conflict was over, a good deal of reflection occurred in Russian military circles. The media, too, were very critical of the overall performance. As Makarov put it, "We had serious drawbacks in the conflict and learned a number of lessons. We will deal with them as soon as possible."[39] Now, though, Serdyukov and Makarov had their chance to push through the reforms that had, heretofore, been stymied by the conservative generals. The conflict with Georgia changed the dynamic where military reform was concerned. Once the war was over and it became clear just how badly the Russian military had performed, then the need for quite drastic reform became starkly evident—even to the conservative generals. Their opposition largely crumbled. Sensing their chance, Serdyukov and Makarov redoubled their efforts to push through the reforms they wished to see.

The first target, again, was the number of superfluous personnel in the military. After the war, the pace of the personnel cuts accelerated. Originally, the armed forces were supposed to reduce in size from 1.3 million down to one million by 2016, 150,000 of whom would be officers. In September 2008, it was announced that such a reducation was now to be achieved by 2012.[40] The second principal target of Serdyukov and Makarov was the basic structural arrangement of the army.

NEW COMMAND STRUCTURES

Perhaps the most obvious reform affecting the army itself related to the introduction of a range of new command structures. These were designed to increase the army's flexibility and to create better command and control arrangements. In October 2008 it was announced that all of the ground forces' divisions were to be converted into brigades, that new command tiers were to come into operation, and that the Military District system was to change to become one of Strategic Commands.[41]

Divisions to Brigades

The war with Georgia made clear that the overall structure of the ground forces was ill-suited to the conduct of modern warfare. To start with, the traditional Russian division of about 10,000 personnel[42] was seen to be a poor basic building block. It did not have the adroitness or flexibility to cope with the demands of fast-moving modern conflict. This was principally because the divisions were top-heavy. They normally consisted of three regiments that could be armored, armored infantry, or basic infantry, depending on the type of division. But the division was a structure suited to all-out conventional warfare as envisaged by all the major potential protagonists during the Cold War. It had the requisite heavy weaponry and a degree of independence supplied by its organic combat support (e.g., artillery) and combat service support (e.g., logistics) assets. Most of these assets would be held at the division level and then released down to the regiments as required. This is what made them top-heavy. Once the Cold War was over, though, Western armies—such as those of the United States and the UK—realized that the division was too large and unwieldy a formation for the expeditionary operations that were in vogue post-1989. The United States and UK both adopted the brigade as the new basic army building-block during the 1990s.[43] Roughly a third of the size of a division and with generally lighter equipment, it could have access to those support assets that were previously held at division level. A brigade was also a more manageable structure in terms of command and control and provided increased flexibility. It could be fairly easily deployed by sea or air within a short period of time and would be immediately able to fight once in theatre and without requiring external aid—barring some air power assets, which the brigade would probably have trained with before any overseas deployment. In the U.S. and British armies, the brigade had become the new formation of choice. It was the future.

Only now were the Russian ground forces catching up. As Serdyukov put it, compared to the division, "the brigade structure is more flexible, mobile and modern."[44] The new brigades, two or two-and-ahalf times larger than the old divisional regiments in terms of numbers, were to mirror Western practice in being modular and having their own combat support and combat service support assets. They could operate independently. Of course, the officers selected to command these new brigades had to get used to the idea of operating independently and in controlling new assets. This was something of a problem in the centralized Russian military system, but many officers did have experience commanding such units as the reinforced battalions that had been sent to Chechnya.[45]

The role of armor in the Soviet/Russian military mindset was also changing. While tank battalions obviously still figure in the Motor Rifle Brigades, only two of the 83 brigades are purely tank brigades. Makarov explains this by saying that "in both future wars and even ones that are occuring now, the role of tanks will be secondary."[46]

The change from divisions to brigades did not take place throughout the army. The airborne forces managed to fend off such a change. The 203 divisions of the ground forces, however, were duly converted into 83 brigades. The only ground force division to be preserved was a machine gun division based in the Kurile Islands.[47] This whole structural rearrangement was put together over a year or so (the conversion was stated to be complete by December 2009). The new brigades were then all deemed to be at "permanent readiness."[48]

This permanent readiness idea resulted from the tardiness of the ground forces units in making their initial moves in the conflict with Georgia. To correct this, in October 2008 Medvedev had called for all formations in the army to be in a state of "permanent combat readiness" by 2012. This was also seen as another signal from the politicians that the practice of conscription should end. Basically, permanent combat readiness could only be achieved by having fully constituted units that could engage in operations without having to wait until they had received their quota of recalled conscripts. Of course, without the need to recall conscripts, there was no need for the mobilization system. It would have to end; or at least be cut back markedly. As military analyst Mikhail Barabanov put it, "Thus, the Russian army basically will cease to be a mobilization army."[49]

What exactly the term "permanent readiness" actually meant was open to debate. Both Makarov and Deputy Defense Minister Nikolai Pankov stated that each of the 83 brigades (with personnel strength of 4,500-5,000) "will be ready for combat within an hour" of getting any order to deploy. This seemed remarkable. Colonel-General Aleksandr Postnikov, the current commander of the ground forces and another of those brought in from Siberia,[50] has said that the term means that the brigades can leave their barracks gate within an hour but would not be capable of combat operations until 24 hours had passed.[51] The head of the (then) Volga-Urals Military District, Lieutenant-General Arkadiy Bakhin, said that the term meant that the brigade had 100 percent manning, 100 percent availability of stores and equipment, and that deployment would be "in that normative time which the General Staff has determined for us to go out . . . within an hour." He confirmed thus the move within an hour.[52] Other military officials have said that it means "capable of going into battle within 1 or 2 hours."[53] Yet other, perhaps more thoughtful, voices have stated that what "permanent readiness" actually means is that the brigades are really no more than fully manned and thus not reliant on conscript recalls.[54]

Some of the brigades are destined to be split into light and heavy variants. One of the brigades in each of the Military Districts (soon to be the four Strategic Commands) is designated as an air assault brigade. As such, it will act as the regional rapid reaction force.[55] It will, however, only ever be delivered by helicopter, and such brigades are not part of the airborne forces; although their personnel are to be trained by the Airborne personnel.[56] The ownership of the helicopter fleet is currently an issue within the Russian military. In 2003 all of the ground forces helicopters were handed over to the control of the Air Force. But the Air Force, dominated as it is by a fast-jet culture, is perceived to have not looked after the helicopter fleet; treating it as an unwelcome step-child. This has meant that the ground forces have not had access to the number of helicopters that they would like, and it is thus proving difficult to train the new air assault brigades.[57]

New Command Tiers

The demise of the division in Russian army thinking also allowed Serdyukov to announce once more, in October 2008, a move designed to help overall command and control procedures. The previous command tiers were arranged as such: Military DistrictArmy-Division-Regiment. This was to be replaced by the new order: Military District-Operational Command-Brigade. This reordering was again designed to increase flexibility. The removal of the Army level meant one less stratum of command and thus a more streamlined system. All of the Military Districts were converted to the tier system on December 1, 2009.[58]

Strategic Commands

The structural reforms went further. It was officially announced in July 2010 that Russia's six Military Districts, dating from the Soviet era, would also be downsized into just four Strategic Commands. These four new Commands—West, East, South, and Central — are replacing the Moscow, Leningrad, Siberia, Far East, Volga-Urals, and North Caucasus Military Districts.[59] The Commands will also provide for better command and control over what have become, since the Soviet period, very much smaller Russian armed forces. They will also be broader in scope. One control center in each Command will now direct not just the ground forces formations, but also navy and air force assets held within the command area. Additionally, and unusually, the commands will also have operational control over the troops of the Interior Ministry, the Emergency Situations Ministry, and the Border Guards stationed within the command.[60] The only units not to be controlled by the Strategic Command headquarters will be those of the Strategic Missile Troops and the Space Troops. Both are still directed centrally from Moscow.

This move from Military Districts to Strategic Commands has also allowed the political masters to make personnel changes that suit their purposes. This is obvious from the choice of the men appointed to head these new Commands. All four are considered to be supporters of reform, and all once served under or with Makarov in the Siberian Military District: Colonel-General Arkady Bakhin in the West; Lieutenant-General Alexsandr Galkin in the South; Admiral Konstantin Sidenko in the East (he was formerly commander of the Pacific Fleet), and Lieutenant-General Vladimir Chirkin assumed control in the Central Strategic Command. Again, these men, like Makarov, are not from the Moscow inner circle of influential General Staff officers. They are also, crucially, men that Makarov trusts.[61]

The East Strategic Command

While the South Strategic Command looks as if it will be the most operationally busy in terms of dealing with terrorist/insurgent issues in the North Caucasus, it is probably the East

Strategic Command that will, in a strategic sense, become the most important. This is because it faces China.

For the Russians, there is certainly some concern about China as a possible future threat; certainly more so than any threat emanating from the United States or the North Atlantic Treaty Organization (NATO). In recent years Russia has experienced a significant influx of Chinese migrants into its underpopulated Far East region. This has raised nationalist issues of a "takeover by stealth" by Beijing of an area of Russia that is rich in the resources that the Chinese economy needs. Moreover, the Chinese military has recently conducted large-scale exercises involving the movement of significant force elements overland for long distances (hundreds of kilometers). This is seen in Moscow as preparation for operations inside Russian territory. Among other responses to this perceived threat, in March 2010, the head of the Siberian Military District moved two ground forces brigades closer to the Chinese border near Chita.[62]

It is, however, very rare for any military figure or government official to actually mention China as a threat by name. Doctrinal statements and national security strategies will, for instance, openly talk of NATO being a "threat" or a "danger" (even though most Russian officials believe this not to be the case), while China is never mentioned or even alluded to.[63] As Jacob Kipp puts it, "The silence about the rise of China and its implications for Moscow has been deafening."[64] Moscow, while believing that the United States, NATO, and Japan can absorb a threatening tone from Moscow with a fair degree of equanimity, does not want to antagonize China: it is, after all, a major trading partner of Russia and occasionally an important diplomatic ally.

Historically, the Far East region has never really figured as a major Russian strategic concern. It was always a military backwater. All of the Soviet Union's best troops and equipment faced west and not east or south. And despite the threat felt now from China, even in 2010 the Far East Military District still contained military formations that were a cause of concern. In January 2010 an inspection had rated the whole Far East Military District as "unsatisfactory," and none of its brigades were judged to be combat ready.[65]

The concentration, though, is now changing. The largest Russian military exercise held since the end of the Cold War, *Vostok-2010*, took place in the late summer of 2010 in the Far East. It involved land, sea, and air elements.[66] And while the point of the exercise was rather bizarrely stated as being to practice dealing with a "terrorist incursion," it clearly concerned the conduct of large-scale conflict.[67] It seems also to have been intended as a warning to China that Russia was ready for any conflict in the region.[68] It was also, of course, a test exercise for the new Far East Strategic Command itself, for the new brigade structures, and for the fledgling NCC currently being developed for the Russian military.[69]

However, even though this exercise was clearly aimed at countering a notional Chinese invasion, the rhetoric of Russian officials said otherwise. Ground troops were taking part, it was made known, to practice dealing with any mass influx of refugees from North Korea. Anti-aircraft systems (S-300s) were involved in order, it was said, to practice engaging pieces of supposedly malfunctioning North Korean rockets, which could fall on Russian territory. Warships were stated to be involved in order to practice countering U.S. naval assets. An amphibious landing was also conducted in the Kurile Islands: this naturally drew Japanese ire and not that of China, the probable real target. None of the elements of *Vostok-2010* were confirmed as being directed at what was clearly the real adversary— the Chinese People's Liberation Army (PLA).[70]

There is, however, a problem with converting from divisions to brigades when facing such a potential enemy as the PLA. The real requirement, if the PLA is to be a future opponent, is for bulky and hard-hitting divisions. "The border with Finland and Norway," as one analyst of the Russian military puts it, "is one thing and that with China is quite another."[71] Brigades, for all their flexibility and speed of response in a complex and compact theater of operations, could, as another observer noted, "simply be lost" in the vast tracts of land in the Far East. Divisions would appear to be the formation of choice for operations that would doubtless be conducted over lengthy periods and require that the engaged formations have access to substantial amounts of organic combat support and combat service support.[72]

It has been stated that the army will deal with any enemy incursion into the Far East first with immediate-use airborne forces, then with the East Strategic Command's own ground forces air assault brigade, and finally with other ground forces brigades that will then be capable of being brought into action. The army leadership understands that the forces currently available in the Far East will not stop any serious PLA invasion. Thus the plan seems to be that if such an invasion cannot be stopped or slowed down sufficiently using brigade elements, then, if there is no alternative, tactical nuclear weapons will be used. Indeed, during *Vostok-2010*, several nuclear land mines were notionally exploded and two Tochka-U (SS-21) missiles, which can carry tactical nuclear warheads, were launched.[73]

Interestingly, reinforcing from the west was also tested during *Vostok-2010*. As part of the exercise, the 28th Motor Rifle Brigade was moved from European Russia to the Far East to test the actual deployability of a brigade. However, instead of deploying with its own heavy equipment, the brigade used tanks and APCs that were waiting in the Far East. This equipment originally belonged to one of the cadre formations that had been disbanded in the recent reforms.[74] This approach appears to have been used because long brigade moves had gone wrong in the previous year's major exercise, *Zapad-2 009*, held in the west of Russia.[75] Su-24M and Su-34 aircraft were also sent from European Russia to the Far East exercise zone accompanied by air-to-air refueling tankers, a critically short Russian military capability.[76] Such lengthy moves by either ground or air assets have never been attempted before in Russian military exercises. Such procedures, along with others practiced in *Vostok-2010*, are helping the Russians write new field manuals.[77]

An important issue in regard to the new emphasis on the Far East region is that it is so different—in terms of topography, climate, and infrastructure development — from other Military Districts or Strategic Command areas. A quite different kind of operational thinking and equipment schedules are needed in the Far East compared to those of military formations operating in the west or the south. It may be, and it is currently being discussed, that Russia may have to develop two different armies—one for the Far East and the other to operate elsewhere.

THE FAILURE OF PROFESSIONALIZATION

One of the main drivers of professionalization in the past was the perceived need to create a body of men who could conduct military operations, while leaving the conscripts to sit quietly in a barracks somewhere out of harm's way. This worked to a large degree in that the vast majority of soldiers going to Chechnya by the 2000s were *kontraktniki*. But today the army has fewer *kontraktniki* than it did in the early to mid-2000s. For example, there are no longer enough *kontraktniki* to man units in such current hotspots as Dagestan and Ingushetia, and operations in Chechnya are now conducted only by local troops of the pro-Moscow government in Grozny.[78] Thus conscripts are still being sent on active service, even though promises were made that they would not.[79] Indeed, in the war with Georgia, 30 percent of the troops involved were conscripts, some of whom were killed during the conflict. These had either been in the original peacekeeping force in South Ossetia, were in the 58th Army, or were part of the airborne forces, all of which should technically have been made up exclusively of *kontraktniki*.[80] Clearly, such deaths indicated that professionalization was not progressing as well as it might.

A further sign that all was not as it should be with the process came in August 2009 when it was announced that the 76th Air Assault Division was never going to be able to be fully professional. Back in 1996, as part of Yeltsin's edict, the 76th had been chosen as the formation that would be the very first to be fully contractualized. Now it was admitted that even this formation had not attracted enough professionals.[81]

The target set for 2008 of having 148,000 *kontraktniki* was thus missed by a wide margin. As Smirnov said, only 100,000 had signed up by January 2008. This figure was for the military overall; i.e., such elements as the ground forces, airborne forces, navy (which is now manned entirely by professionals[82]), air force, space troops, and strategic rocket forces. The situation has now worsened. In January 2009, Smirnov announced that there were only 79,000 *kontraktniki* in the military,[83] although the most recent figure quoted puts the number at 90,000.[84]

There are many reasons why the professionalization program ran into problems. Obviously, the generals were throwing their spanners into the works, but there was more to it than that. The initial promises on pay and housing had not been kept. Thus those who had signed on as *kontraktniki* were not inclined to continue their service beyond 3 years, and those who were tempted to join up were put off and changed their minds. There were also budgetary constraints. While the state was not paying the *kontraktniki* much, it could only afford to pay for a finite number.[85] Nonetheless, it is difficult to say what the exact reasons are for the failure to achieve the target number of *kontraktniki*.

In February 2010 Makarov, citing the cost factor, officially deemed the whole professionalization process to be a failure. Although it was his opinion that the "best option is to have a totally contract army,"[86] he now had to accept the inevitable. "Very many mistakes were made," he said, "and the task set of building professional armed forces has not been accomplished. Therefore the decision has been made that conscript service must remain in the armed forces. . . . We are not going to go over to a contract basis. Moreover, we are increasing the draft and reducing the contract part."[87] In April 2010, Makarov stated that Russia would never totally get rid of conscription. Thus, the country will continue with the system for the foreseeable future, ending the political hopes that it could be abandoned. It appears now that, in both the ground forces and the airborne forces, the concept of mixed-manning has emerged. That is, there will be no completely professional units: all will have a mixture of the two types (except for some special forces units and detachments, which will be totally professional). All of the newly formed brigades will have some complement of *kontraktniki,* although this is likely to vary among brigades with some more permanently ready if they contain more *kontraktniki*.

In the current army, some 20 percent of personnel are said to be professionals.[88] Most of these are more likely to occupy the more technical branches, such as air defense, artillery, and signals. In infantry units, such positions as commanders, gunners, and drivers of APCs would normally be *kontraktniki*, while the rest of the squad/section would be conscripts.[89]

In essence, the failure of professionalization is a victory for the conservative generals who all along had done their best to thwart the move towards professionalization. As Golts sums up, "The sad story of the [move to contract manning] is a classic example of how . . . officials can upset any reform that is not to their advantage."[90] Golts, indeed, lays the blame squarely on Colonel-General Smirnov, the Deputy CGS.[91]

However, while the whole professionalization process has not been an unalloyed success, and although this might be seen as a victory of sorts by many in the military hierarchy, it is something of a Pyrrhic one, for the army, as well as the rest of the military, must now accept the concept of conscripts who serve for only 1 year.[92]

The first problem with such conscripts is obviously the lack of time they spend with their ascribed units. After his 3-month training stint (or 6 months if the individual is destined for a technical branch of the military), the conscript will only ever spend some 9 months in his unit. As such, he is more a liability than an asset. Moreover, such men are not in their units long enough to take part in any annual field exercises. It is quite common now for conscripts to have their terms extended so they can take part in such exercises. Remarkably, some 50 percent of the 20,000 servicemen who took part in the Vostok-2010 major exercise in September 2010 had only just been called up in that spring's conscription draft. Thus half of the troops involved in the Russian military's biggest exercise since the end of the Cold War had served for less than 6 months. Some of them, technically, were still in training.[93] The implications for the military's combat potential are clear.

The second problem with the 1-year term is that since the length of conscript service has been halved (from 2 years to 1), then double the number of conscripts must now be brought into the military to maintain the troop strength demanded by the generals. Thus the call-ups now held in the spring and fall of every year that were previously bringing in just 260,000 or so young men per annum now must at least double such figures. So to bring in the 500,000-600,000 conscripts now needed every year by the military obviously means that the conscription net has had to be spread much wider. Men previously exempt, such as those with very young children, college graduates, or doctors, are now being asked to present themselves for service.[94] The scale of medical deferments has also been markedly reduced, while those with a criminal record can now also serve as conscripts.[95] All this widening of the net has had to take place against a background of new constrictions on the availability of potential conscripts caused by both falling health standards and a falling birth-rate in Russia. Of the 400,000 young men currently leaving high school every year, a third are deemed to be unfit for military service.[96] In all of 2002, for instance, 335,000 men were conscripted out of a total population of 145.2 million. In 2008, it was 334,000 out of a population of 142 million. In 2009, it was 625,000 out of an as yet unknown population— but certainly one smaller than in 2008. The mathematics are problematic: if only 400,000 young men leave school every year, how long can the military continue to conscript 600,000 and more per annum? And of course, all of these new problems with the 1-year term can be added to the traditional draft avoidance issues surrounding the Russian conscription system. (Estimates are that 130,000 men are currently dodging the draft.[97])

It must be assumed that if the conscription net is being spread wider and wider, then two contrasting features should be apparent. The first is that if more educated men can now be called up, then the average intelligence of the Russian conscript must be increasing—helpful when complicated military technologies have to be handled. On the other hand, more men must be called up who really do object to being part of a military organization. Such men can become troublemakers and upset unit morale.[98]

Moreover, with such huge numbers of conscripts now being brought into the military every year, a similarly huge number of troops then become tied down in either training this number or in simply transporting them from location to location. Experienced personnel are thus removed from the operational order of battle.[99]

A fourth problem is "churn," or turnover, within units. Every spring and fall when the conscript call-ups take place, units lose some 50 percent of their personnel and have to accept a massive new intake. Unit cohesion must inevitably suffer.[100]

The shortage of conscripts is certainly not due to a lack of effort on the part of the recruiting offices, or commissariats. These commissariats, which fall under the control of Colonel-General Smirnov, have been given quotas for bringing in conscripts.[101] Monetary rewards are handed out when an office meets or exceeds its quota. The doctors performing the entry medicals are likewise rewarded. It is thus no surprise if some sharp practice is entered into in order to meet these quotas. Some of this activity amounts to press-ganging. As one analyst points out, "Cases are known in which a young man has gone off to his place of work or education in the morning and has found himself in a military unit by that evening. Everything is done in a day, so the youth is unable to contest his illegal induction." It seems that even if the conscript is medically unfit for service, it is not the commissariat's problem. If he is found to be unfit once he gets to his training unit, then he will still have been registered and thus will have helped to fulfil the commissariat's target.[102]

The army is desperate to have more conscripts. If any of the brigades are not fully manned using conscripts, then they will lose their permanent readiness status and thus receive a poor inspection rating.[103] Smirnov is currently trying to increase the military's share of the conscript intake by reducing the number going to other agencies. He does not want to see any conscripts being sent to organizations such as the Foreign Intelligence Service (SVR),[104] and he wants a reduction in the numbers going to the Interior Ministry (MVD) and the Emergency Services Ministry (EMERCOM).[105]

It may now be the case that the conscript term will have to go back up to 2 years. This will be pushed by the military but resisted by the politicians. It is sure to generate public protest. So the army, at least for the time being (and at least until after the presidential elections of 2012), will have to deal with a series of problems being created by the fact that the conscription term is only 1 year.

With the massive cutback in officer numbers and the closing of the cadre formation bases across Russia, it is obvious now that the mobilization system can no longer function as it once did. It has been estimated that the whole Russian military will now, in a time of crisis, only have the capacity to call up some 700,000 reservists. This would take the military up to a personnel strength of 1.7 million. What the size of the ground forces itself would be on mobilization is, like many aspects related to the study of the Russian military, not clear. But it is clear that virtually all of the recalled conscripts will be those who have only served for 1 year.[106]

The relatively small size of this mobilized military is raising some disquiet; particularly in relation to the fact that Russia may not be able to defend itself with conventional means and will therefore have to employ tactical nuclear weapons. As Konstantin Sivkov, retired from the General Staff's Centre for Military- Strategic Studies, argues:

> The elimination of cadre units will strike a terrible blow against the country's defence capabilities. The result is that when a threat escalates from armed conflict to local war, we will have to go over to the use of nuclear weapons.[107]

Such a warning—and others made by like-minded individuals—may, however, merely represent a scare tactic by those who wish to ensure that the overall size of the military does not drop too far.[108]

EDUCATION AND TRAINING

There is a natural tension within a Russian military manned largely by short-service conscripts that is also being called upon to modernize and become an effective fighting force. A number of reforms have had to take place in order to deal with this issue.

Military Training in Schools

One way chosen to alleviate the problems caused by the 1-year term of conscription, and announced in a February 2010 decree, has been to resurrect the Soviet concept of the Voluntary Association for Assistance to the Army, Air Force, and Navy (DOSAAF). Under this system, retired officers used to prepare high school children for conscript service. The training/indoctrination sometimes involved work in classrooms and sometimes in the field on camping trips. The subjects taught were mostly benign military skills, such as fieldcraft, map reading, and using radios.[109] The plan was that by the time the pupils had reached conscription age, they would already have had a basic introduction to military skills.[110]

The new version of DOSAAF, and very similar to it, is known as the Russian Defence Sports-Technical Organization (ROSTO).[111] Planned to be allied to ROSTO, and sometimes running concurrently with it, is another new system whereby pre-draft-age young men spend time at pre-conscription training centers. These are to be established in all Russian regions beginning in 2011. Up to 15,000 retired officers (many just having been made redundant) are earmarked to do the training—which will doubtless involve more technical military skills.[112] Moreover, high schools will soon teach military subjects as part of their overall curricula.[113]

The advent of ROSTO and pre-conscription training is evidence that Russia still harbors a desire to hold on to the citizen army concept—implying that mass still has a place in Russian military thinking. How this concept squares with the accepted military logic of having highly trained professional soldiers operating modern high-tech military equipment is difficult to fathom. It can only make sense if China, with its PLA relying on mass, is seen as the most likely future enemy.

Non-Commissioned Officers

Any army needs a decent corps of NCOs: personnel with military skills, with leadership ability, and, most of all, with *experience*. The former 2-year conscript term of service, while it still meant that soldiers could never serve long enough to develop true NCO capabilities, could at least justify the promotion of a number of conscripts to become NCOs (*serzhanti*[114]) for the last 6 months of their term. While this produced some junior leadership, it could not deal with the issue of troops having to man modern, sophisticated military equipment. The traditional Soviet approach — a legacy necessarily passed on to the Russian military—was to supply its conscript troops with very basic equipment that even a Central Asian peasant who did not speak Russian could work with. The aim was to keep everything simple, but the whole current military modernization project naturally has to involve a move away from simplicity. The lack of proper NCOs has thus been highlighted and become a particular concern as military technology has improved.

Another traditional Soviet approach was to let the officers take on many of the tasks that would normally fall to junior NCOs in Western armies. The Russian army also inherited this characteristic. If nothing else, it provided an argument to political masters against cutting officer posts. Moreover, given that the conscript term is now only 1 year, today's Russian officers are being called on to undertake even more of the basic tasks that should really be within the purview of NCOs. Officers are thus not doing what they should be doing—improving their own officer skills.

Initially, when *kontraktniki* first started to come into the army in the mid-1990s, the General Staff objected to them being trained to become NCOs. Such professional NCOs would have undermined the generals' argument that officers were needed, in part, to do the jobs of NCOs. They had made sure that there was no program to train the NCOs that would make the system work.[115]

Again, though, the conflict with Georgia undermined this argument by opening the inadequacies of the army to public scrutiny, and one of the obvious inadequacies was the fact that junior leadership was lacking. And this problem was not helped by the announced cutback in officer numbers and the elimination of the rank of warrant officer. There is thus now a shortage of both to do the NCO tasks. Some units are currently reported to be unmanageable due to a dearth of proper leadership.[116] In an effort to get around this obvious lacuna, the General Staff has decided to take 5,000 young officers fresh from military academies and to put them into NCO positions. Thus the previously unofficial and unacknowledged system whereby officers were doing NCOs jobs has now become official. These men—paid as officers—have been promised that they will assume real officer appointments at the first opportunity.[117]

The fall-out from the war with Georgia also meant that the establishment of a proper system of NCO development could no longer be resisted. Serdyukov was thus able to establish a new training school specifically for NCOs — the first in Russia since the Tsarist era.[118] This was to be based at the main training base of the airborne forces in Ryazan. The airborne forces had come out of the Georgian conflict with their reputation actually enhanced, and not diminished as with the ground forces, and so they were chosen to train all of the army's NCOs. It is hoped by Serdyukov that some of the airborne's *esprit de corps* and fighting spirit will rub off on the new NCOs.

A 3-year NCO training program is now running at Ryazan. The personnel chosen to go to there are recruited from those aged 19-35 who have already completed at least a year of service (either as a conscript or professional), who have completed secondary education, and who have agreed to sign on for 5 years' service once they have graduated from the school. Recruits for NCO training are also being sought in the reserves. The first graduates will appear in 2012, and will naturally assume the posts of quite senior NCOs, equivalent to sergeants and staff sergeants in the West. Their arrival will definitely increase the combat capability of all Russian army units—both airborne and ground forces.[119]

There are some teething problems with this new means of creating NCOs. One is the sheer expense, in Russian military terms, of running this new course. Another is the scale of the problem. The Russian army needs tens of thousands of NCOs and not just the 250 or so per year the current scheme will produce for the 35,000-strong airborne forces and the approximately 400,000 in the ground forces.[120] Ryazan therefore merely represents a drop in the ocean. As one analyst notes, "the creation of such an NCO corps even under the most favourable conditions will not require 3 to 4 years, but no fewer than 10-15. This delay potentially creates a threat to the announced reforms."[121] The realization that an effective NCO system cannot be created overnight has reportedly led to a halt in the removal of the rank of warrant officer, and those of that rank slated to be made redundant are now being kept in the military.[122]

Officer Training

Serdyukov's plan is to close a good proportion of the 72 officer academies. These used to turn out some 18,000 officers a year (including 7,500 conscript officers). The plan now is to train only 1,500-2000 officers annually (with no conscript officers[123]) in a greatly reduced number of academies.[124]

EQUIPMENT

As noted, it is not the purpose here to produce a detailed account of technical improvements under the current Russian Army modernization process. This is partly a reflection of the fact that there have simply not been many such improvements. Recent statements on Russian military spending indicate that strategic nuclear, air force, and air defense forces have a higher priority than the ground forces.[125] The Russian army's equipment is still basically that of the Soviet army, with a few updates to old frames. Tanks, for instance, have not been a major target of investment.

There is deemed to be no real need to build newer models. Tanks were lost in the war with Georgia mostly because they had not been properly prepared for battle, and not because they were unfit for battle. It is the same with APCs, although foreign (wheeled) APCs are being purchased. As with Western armies, the Russian army is moving more towards employing wheeled APCs because of their increased deploy- ability and flexibility compared to tracked variants.[126] In Russia, however, wheeled APCs have been recognized as unsuitable for use in the Far East where the road system is underdeveloped. Again, there is the issue of the two armies: one with equipment for the west and south of Russia and one with equipment for the Far East. The army is also procuring from abroad several tactical-level systems such as unmanned aerial vehicles (UAVs) for reconnaissance, sniper rifles, armored vests, and night-vision goggles to fill obvious gaps exposed by the war with Georgia.[127]

It has been pointed out in Russia that the lack of a modern command and control system is "the principal problem with the Russian Army."[128] This is also slowly being dealt with. More tactical radios are being issued at squad level and better interservice means of communication are being developed. A rudimentary NCC is also being introduced and has been tested in a few exercises, but it is nowhere near the capability of Western analogues. The current reduction in both horizontal and vertical command levels with the introduction of the new command tiers and the Strategic Command concept should ease the proposed intro-duction of the NCC into the armed forces.[129] As would be expected, however, such systems are proving difficult for Russian officers to master, from both cultural and technical aspects.[130]

The politicians have promised to provide the military with the most modern weapons, apparently as a sop to the generals to sweeten the bitter pill of the overall cutbacks. But many such modern weapons can only be procured from abroad because the Russian defense industry is more in need of modernizing than the military itself. As noted, the Russian military- industrial complex can really only produce updated systems from Soviet times. High-tech systems and assets that are commonplace in Western militaries simply cannot be produced in Russia.[131]

THE MODERNIZATION PROCESS

It is quite difficult, given the conflicting data available , to establish just how far the process of Russian military modernization has come and where exactly this leaves the ground forces. However, a few main points can be made:

- The Russian military will probably never be totally professional.
- As things currently stand, the personnel strength of the military is in the region of 1.1 million. The ground forces strength is probably between 350,000 and 400,000.
- The military's command and control structures have been simplified, and there will undoubtedly be better future coordination between the services and among the services.
- Better communications systems are being introduced into the ground forces at all levels. This will alleviate the command and control issues that emerged in the war with Georgia.
- The military education structures are also being streamlined, and the new NCO school will inevitably help create—no matter how small—a corps of well-trained and effective NCOs.
- The ground forces may now actually be *short* of officers if it is accepted that they perform a variety of NCO functions. Since there are no "real" NCOs yet to take over from the now absent officers, units are bound to miss such officers.

- The elimination of the rank of warrant officer appears to have been halted. The posts of some warrant officers have, however, already been contracted out to civilians.
- Despite all the changes made in the Russian ground forces, its units are not suddenly going to become highly effective. There will still be far too many short-service conscripts in their ranks and not enough NCOs. The officers will still have their skill sets limited by all the mundane tasks that they have to perform. If the need is for rapid-reaction capabilities, or if an expeditionary operation needs to be conducted, then it is the airborne forces that will be called upon, not the ground forces.
- So long as it does not prove too expensive, the probability is that two Russian armies will form: one to conduct operations in the south and west of the country and another to conduct operations in the Far East. The equipment and the education/training of both officers and other ranks will be different for each army.
- The only likely change in ground forces heavy equipment for the foreseeable future is that more wheeled vehicles will be procured from abroad. Very few upgraded main battle tanks are likely to be delivered in the coming years.
- Ground forces are being created that will be more suitable for use against small-scale opponents than against NATO or China.
- The claim that ground force units can be on the move within an hour of a call-out is very debatable.
- Ground force units will be very much weakened by the fact that twice a year they lose almost 50 percent of their personnel.
- It remains to be seen just how the ground forces will adjust to the new brigade structure. Exercises are reported to have gone well when they have involved the brigades. But to what degree such claims can be believed remains moot.
- Their use of tactical nuclear weapons cannot be ruled out in any future engagement between Russian and Chinese forces.

Conclusion

Russia's political leaders are currently pushing a state- and society-wide process of modernization. But such a process takes time. There can be no overnight solutions. So it is with the modernization of the Russian military. It all seems to be rushed. The radical changes that have been both proposed and introduced need to be given time to embed. For while new structures can be created and new equipment and technologies procured, the crucial element in such changes is the degree to which they are accepted by the human element. This is often the most difficult aspect in any process of organizational change. The Russian military is a deeply conservative institution, and it is being asked to accept fundamental changes. Changes, indeed, that threaten the very livelihoods of those being asked to implement them. It is no wonder that the military modernization process is progressing slowly in Russia. The Russian ground forces will not be very different in the next few years than they are now. Time and future investment will eventually produce the more refined army that a host of Russian politicians have wished to see. But it will take time and investment.

End Notes

[1] See Rod Thornton, "Military Organizations and Change: The 'Prof essionalization' of the 76th Airborne Division," *Journal of Slavic Military Studies*, Vol. 17, No. 3, 2004, pp. 449-474.

[2] He is also Chief of Staff of the Main Organization and Mobilization Directorate.

[3] Nikolai Krasnykh, "Servicemen intend to fight for draft," *Moscow KM-Novosti*, June 24, 2009, quoted on *BBC Monitoring* (hereinafter BBC Mon) *FS1 FsuPol sv/osc.*

[4] *RIA Novosti* press release, "Russian Military Denies Problems with Conscription," April 4, 2010, available from *en.rian.ru/ military_news/20100401/158396990.htm*l.

[5] Mikhail Yakovlev, "Breach of Contract: Will the Defense Ministry Give up the Transition to a Professional Army?" *Nasha Versiya*, March 1, 2010, quoted on BBC Monitoring World Media Monitor, available from *BBC Mon FS1 FsuPol 050310 nn/osc.*

[6] Thornton, "Military Organizations and Change."

[7] Aleksandr Golts, "Not a Step Forward," *Novaya Vremya*, August 31, 2009, quoted on *BBC Mon FS1 FsuPol 020909 ysk/osc.*

[8] Yuriy Gavrilov, "Interview with Chief of the General Staff Makarov," *Rossiyskaya Gazeta*, March 23, 2010, p. 7.

[9] Thornton, "Military Organizations and Change."

[10] Nikolai Pavlovskiy, "Goodbye, Soviet Army," *Boss Magazine*, February 15, 2010, quoted in *BBC Mon FS1 FsuPol 010310 emergency/osc.*

[11] *Ibid.*

[12] Gavrilov, "Interview with Chief of the General Staff Makarov."

[13] *Ibid.*

[14] *Ibid.*

[15] *Ibid.*

[16] *Federalnaya Sluzba Bezopasnosti* (Federal Service of Security). Akin to the FBI or MI5.

[17] In a speech to the Federal Assembly in 2007; Golts, "Not a Step Forward."

[18] Yuliy Estinko, "Realities: Commanders are Being Seated at the School Desk," *Nezavisimoye Voyennoye Obozreniye*, March 5, 2010, quoted on *BBC Mon FS1 FsuPol 070310 nn/osc.*

[19] Nikolai Poroskov, "Draft Obsession," *Vremya Novostey*, March 31, 2010, p. 4.

[20] Alexander Golts, "In Uniform: Tanks Are Not Afraid of Snow," *Yezhednevnyy Zhurnal* website, March 1, 2010, quoted on *BBC Mon FsuPol 040310 ak/osc.*

[21] Ruslan Pukhov, "Serdyukov Cleans Up the Arbat," *Moscow Defense Brief*, January 15, 2009.

[22] Vladimir Mukhin, "Catastrophic Look of the Russian Army," *Nezavisimoye Voyennoye Obozreniye*, January 18, 2010, p. 2.

[23] Mikhail Leontyev, "Interview with Defense Minister Anatoliy Serdyukov," *Odnako*, February 15, 2010, p. 13.

[24] Pavlovskiy, "Goodbye, Soviet Army."

[25] Leontyev, "Interview with Defence Minister Anatoliy Serdyukov."

[26] Pavlovskiy, "Goodbye, Soviet Army."

[27] *Ibid.*

[28] Olga Bozheva, "Right Dress! Media . . . Dismissed!" *Moksovskiy Komsomolets*, September 11, 2008, p. 4.

[29] Viktor Baranets, "Lessons from the Caucasus: One Year Later,"website of *Komsomolskaya Pravda*, August 6, 2009, quoted on *BBC Mon FS1 FsuPol iu/osc.*

[30] *Ibid.*

[31] Vladimir Mukhin, "The GLONASS is Lacking Satellites," *Nezavisimoye Voyennoye Obozreniye*, September 19, 2008, p. 5.

[32] *RIA Novosti* report, September 11, 2008, quoted on *BBC Mon FS1 FsuPol gyl.*

[33] Baranets, "Lessons from the Caucasus: One Year Later."

[34] "GLONASS Constellation Grows to 17 as Latest Satellites Come On-Line," *Inside GNSS*, November-December 2008, p. 4.

[35] An attempt was made by the Russian military to switch and use the GPS. After 2 days, though, this was "turned off" over Georgia. Mukhin, "The GLONASS is Lacking Satellites."

[36] Leontyev, "Interview with Defence Minister Anatoliy Serdyukov."

[37] Baranets, "Lessons from the Caucasus: One Year Later."

[38] Yuriy Gavrilov, "A Limited Army," *Rossiyskaya Gazeta*, September 9, 2008, p. 6.

[39] *RIA Novosti*, "Russia's General Staff Announces Strategic Drills with Belarus," December 10, 2008, available from *en.rian.ru/ russia/20081210/118785608.html.*

[40] Aleksandr Golts, "A Military Spoiler Doctrine," *The Moscow Times*, December 16, 2008, p. 7.

[41] Dimitry Litovkin, "To All Four Sides: Instead of Military Districts, Russia will have Strategic Commands," *Izvestiya*, April 30, 2010, p. 2.

[42] NATO divisions were normally about 15,000 strong.

[43] A brigade would normally be built around three battalions. These battalions (sometimes called "regiments") would be in some sort of combination of armored, armored infantry, or basic infantry.

[44] Leontyev, "Interview with Defence Minister Anatoliy Serdyukov."

[45] Yuriy Gavrilov, "Rear Echelon Generals to Retire," *Rossiyskaya Gazeta*, January 22, 2009, p. 7.

[46] Gavrilov, "Interview with Chief of the General Staff Makarov."

[47] *Ibid.*

[48] Pavlovskiy, "Goodbye, Soviet Army."

[49] Mikhail Barabanov, "An End to Mobilization?" *Kommersant-Vlast*, October 20, 2008, p. 3.

[50] Postnikov, then head of the Siberian Military District, was appointed commander in chief of ground forces in January 2010.

[51] Golts, "In Uniform: Tanks Are Not Afraid of Snow."

[52] Interview with Lieutenant-General Arkadiy Bakhin, *Radio Echo Moskvy*, March 6, 2010, quoted on *BBC Mon FS1 FsuPol 140310 nn/osc*.

[53] Pavlovskiy, "Goodbye, Soviet Army."

[54] Oleg Gorupay, "Outlines of the New Look," *Krasnaya Zvezda*, February 18, 2010, p. 3.

[55] Gavrilov, "Rear Echelon Generals to Retire," p. 8.

[56] Victor Baranets, "The Airborne Troops Have Been Hit by Reform: The Airborne Troops Tula Division May be Disbanded," *Komsomolskaya Pravda*, October 25, 2008, p. 7.

[57] Anon, "Reforms in the Military," *Zavtra*, March 3, 2010, quoted on *BBC Mon FS1 FsuPol 050310 em/osc*.

[58] Mukhin, "Catastrophic Look of the Russian Army."

[59] Although the name of the city of Leningrad changed back to St. Petersburg after the Cold War, the local region and military district are still referred to as Leningrad.

[60] The Border Guards are part of the FSB.

[61] Roger McDermott, "New Russian Strategic Level Commanders," *Eurasia Daily Monitor*, Vol. 7, No. 149, August 3, 2010.

[62] Roger McDermott, "Reflections on Vostok 2010: Selling an Image," *Eurasia Daily Monitor*, Vol. 7, No. 134, July 13, 2010, available from *www.jamestown.org/single/?no_cacheD=36614.html*.

[63] *Ibid.*

[64] Jacob Kipp, "Russia's Military Doctrine: New Dangers Appear," *Eurasia Daily Monitor*, Vol. 7, No. 35, February 22, 2010, available from *www.jamestown.org/single/?no_cacheD=36073.html*.

[65] Mukhin, "Catastrophic Look of the Russian Army."

[66] *Vostok-2010* was a combined arms operation involving 20,000 men, 40 ships, and 75 aircraft.

[67] Sergei Blagov, "Russia Boosts Far Eastern Security," *Eurasia Daily Monitor*, Vol. 7, No. 137, July 16, 2010, available from *www.jamestown.org/single/?no_cacheD=36630.html*.

[68] Jacob Kipp, "Vostok 2010 and the Very Curious Hypothetical Opponent," *Eurasia Daily Monitor*, Vol. 7, No. 133, available from *www.jamestown.org/single/?no_cacheD=36610.html*.

[69] Roger McDermott, "Russian Military Prepares for Vostok 2010," *The Jamestown Foundation Eurasia Daily Monitor*, Vol. 7, No. 106, June 2, 2010.

[70] McDermott, "Reflections on Vostok 2010: Selling an Image."

[71] Konstantin Chuprin, "Trends: Too Early to Write Off Divisions," *Voenno-Promyshlenny Kuryer* website, February 3, 2010, quoted on *BBC Mon FsuPol 100310 nm/osc*.

[72] "Military Secret," Russian Ren TV Programme, November 1, 2008, quoted in "Russian TV Report Questions Military Reform Blueprint," available from *news.monitor.bbc.co.uk/profile/cgi/ save_as_profile.pl*.

[73] McDermott, "Reflections on Vostok 2010: Selling an Image."

[74] Oleg Falichev, "Vostok-2010: Beginning, Culmination, Epilogue," *Voyenno-Promyshlennyy Kuryer*, July 14, 2010, quoted on *BBC MonFS1 FsuPol 160710 ak/osc*.

[75] It took one Moscow tank brigade 7 days to cover a distance of 900 km in order to reach an exercise area in Belarus. A Chinese division only took 5 days to cover 2,400 km in an exercise in 2009. Anon., "Military Reform Trips Up on Manoeuvres," *Osobaya Bukva* website, January 1, 2010.

[76] Kipp, "Vostok 2010 and the Very Curious Hypothetical Opponent."

[77] Falichev, "Vostok-2010."

[78] Young Chechen men, moreover, are not conscripted into the Russian military, rather they join local militias. Some federal troops garrison Chechnya, but they take no part in any counterterrorist operations.

[79] However, if conscripts are sent to the North Caucasus, they do receive the same salary as *kontraktniki*.

[80] Victor Litovkin, "Realities: Once Again the Draft, Once Again Problems," *Nezavisimoye Voyennoye Obozreniye*, April 9, 2010, p. 4.

[81] Golts, "Not a Step Forward."

[82] Gavrilov, "Interview with Chief of the General Staff Makarov."

[83] Golts, "In Uniform: Tanks Are Not Afraid of Snow."

[84] Yakovlev, "Breach of Contract."

[85] Litovkin, "Realities."

[86] Gavrilov, "Interview with Chief of the General Staff Makarov."

[87] Yakovlev, "Breach of Contract."

[88] Gavrilov, "Interview with Chief of the General Staff Makarov."

[89] Litovkin, "Realities."

[90] Golts, "Not a Step Forward."

[91] Golts, "In Uniform: Tanks Are Not Afraid of Snow."

[92] Poroskov, "Draft Obsession."

[93] McDermott, "Russian Military Prepares for Vostok 2010."

[94] Currently, well over 20 percent of Russian conscripts have college degrees. This is a double-edged sword in that while more intelligent men are called up to serve in the likes of the Strategic Rocket Forces or the Space Troops, the economy suffers because these men are not available to contribute to it.

[95] Some 64 percent of conscripts now serving actually are not medically fit enough to join operational units. Between 2000 and 2008, no one with a criminal record could be conscripted. This restriction has now been relaxed and of the 305,000 called up, for instance, in the spring of 2009, 170,000 had some sort of criminal record.

[96] Poroskov, "Draft Obsession."

[97] "Russian Military Concerned with Evasion as Army Draft, Begins," *Radio Free Europe*, available from *www.rferl.org/content/ Russian_Military_Concerned_With_Evasion_As_Army_Draft_Begins/21 76960.html*.

[98] Krasnykh, "Servicemen Intend to Fight for Draft."

[99] *Ibid*.

[100] Aleksandr Golts, "More Cannon Fodder for the Army," *The Moscow Times*, May 25, 2010, p. 7.

[101] The commissariats are part of the Main Organization and Mobilization Directorate, which Smirnov controls.

[102] Poroskov, "Draft Obsession."

[103] In Defense Ministry inspections in 2009, only three units, the crews of three Northern Fleet nuclear submarines, were rated as "Excellent." Two-thirds of all military units were graded as "satisfactory." In a speech by Lieutenant-General Valeriy Yevnevich, Head of Main Combat Training Directorate, Russian Defence Ministry website, November 30, 2009, quoted on *BBC Mon FS1 FsuPol 051209 nm/osc*.

[104] *Sluzhba Vneshney Razvedki* (Service of External Intelligence).

[105] Vladimir Mukhin, "Academic Leave on Parade," *Nezavisimaya Gazeta*, May 12, 2010, p. 8.

[106] Aleksandr Golts, "U.S. Not a Threat After All," *Moscow Times*, November 18, 2008, p. 6.

[107] Konstantin Sivkov, "An End to Mobilization?" *utro.ru* website at *www.utro.ru/news/2008/10/21/678576.shtml*.

[108] Golts, "U.S. Not a Threat After All."

[109] The decree is called "The Concept of the Federal System for Training RF Citizens for Military Service for the Period up to 2020."

[110] Poroskov, "Draft Obsession."

[111] Denis Telmanov, "Russian Army Transformed into 86 Mobile Brigades," *Gazeta.ru* quoted on *BBC Mon FS1 FsuPol 230210 nn/osc*.

[112] "Pre-conscription DOSAAF Training Centres to Appear in Russian Regions in 2011," Interfax-AVN website, May 24, 2010, quoted on *BBC Mon FS1 FsuPol iu*.

[113] Mukhin, "Academic Leave on Parade."

[114] This word tends to be translated into English as "sergeant" and not "NCO."

[115] Golts, "In Uniform: Tanks Are Not Afraid of Snow."

[116] Anon., "Military Reform Trips Up on Manoeuvres."

[117] Vladimir Bogdanov and Mikhail Falaleyev, "Desperate Draft: Army Ranks Will be Replenished by 30 Year-Olds," *Rossiyskaya Gazeta*, May 4, 2010.

[118] Pavlovskiy, "Goodbye, Soviet Army."

[119] Aleksandr Tikhonov, "The Word "Sergeant" Has a Proud Ring," *Krasnaya Zvezda*, August 18, 2009, p. 7.

[120] Yuliy Estinko, "Realities: Commanders are Being Seated at the School Desk," *Nezavisimoye Voyennoye Obozreniye*, March 5, 2010, quoted on *BBC Mon FS1 FsuPol 070310 nn/osc*. Figures for the number actually in the airborne forces and ground forces are vague.

[121] Barabanov, "An End to Mobilization?'

[122] Pavlovskiy, "Goodbye, Soviet Army."

[123] Krasnykh, "Servicemen Intend to Fight for Draft."

[124] Leontyev, "Interview with Defence Minister Anatoliy Serdyukov."

[125] Dmitry Gorenburg, "Russia's State Armaments Program 2020: Is the Third Time the Charm for Military Modernization?" available from *russiamil.wordpress.com/*.

[126] They are being bought from the Italian firm IVECO initially and will later be produced under licence in Russia. *RIA Novosti*, "Russian Paratroopers to Get New Weaponry— Commander," July 29, 2009, available from *en.rian.ru/military news/20090729/155665326.html*.

[127] Baranets, "Lessons from the Caucasus: One Year Later."

[128] Ilya Kramnik, "The Scale is Impressive, the Problems are Worrying," *Voyenno-Promyshlennyy Kuryer*, July 14, 2010, on *BBC Mon FS1 FsuPol 150710 mk/osc*.

[129] Litovkin, "To All Four Sides."

[130] Baranets, "Lessons from the Caucasus: One Year Later."

[131] Roger McDermott, "Medvedev Contemplates Modernizing the Russian Defense Industry," *Eurasia Daily Monitor*, Vol. 6, No. 202, November 3, 2009.

In: Russian Military: Ground Force Modernization...   ISBN: 978-1-62100-347-2
Editor: Alessandra R. Guardano   © 2012 Nova Science Publishers, Inc.

Chapter 2

THE RUSSIAN MILITARY AND THE GEORGIAN WAR: LESSONS AND IMPLICATIONS[*]

Ariel Cohen and Robert E. Hamilton

The Strategic Studies Institute (SSI) is part of the U.S. Army War College and is the strategic-level study agent for issues related to national security and military strategy with emphasis on geostrategic analysis.

The mission of SSI is to use independent analysis to conduct strategic studies that develop policy recommendations on:

- Strategy, planning, and policy for joint and combined employment of military forces;
- Regional strategic appraisals;
- The nature of land warfare;
- Matters affecting the Army's future;
- The concepts, philosophy, and theory of strategy; and
- Other issues of importance to the leadership of the Army.

Studies produced by civilian and military analysts concern topics having strategic implications for the Army, the Department of Defense, and the larger national security community.

In addition to its studies, SSI publishes special reports on topics of special or immediate interest. These include edited proceedings of conferences and topically-oriented roundtables, expanded trip reports, and quick-reaction responses to senior Army leaders.

The Institute provides a valuable analytical capability within the Army to address strategic and other issues in support of Army participation in national security policy formulation.

---

[*] This is an edited, reformatted and augmented version of a Strategic Studies Institute publication, dated on June 2011.

ERAP MONOGRAPH

FOREWORD

In August 2008, the armed conflict between Russia and Georgia broke out on the territory of Georgia's breakaway regions of South Ossetia and Abkhazia. The Russian-planned military campaign lasted 5 days until the parties reached a preliminary ceasefire agreement on August 12. The European Union (EU), led by the French presidency, mediated the ceasefire. After signing the agreement, Russia pulled most of its troops out of uncontested Georgian territories, but established buffer zones around Abkhazia and South Ossetia.

On August 26, 2008, Russia recognized the independence of South Ossetia and Abkhazia, making them a part of what President Dmitry Medvedev called Moscow's "zone of privileged interests," and since then deploying five military bases on occupied Georgian territory.

In their monograph, Dr. Ariel Cohen and Colonel Robert Hamilton show how Russia won the war against Georgia by analyzing the goals of war, which include the annexation of Abkhazia, the weakening or toppling the Saakashvili regime, and the prevention of NATO enlargement in the Caucasus. The war demonstrated that Russia's military is in need of significant reforms and it indicated which of those reforms are currently being implemented. Finally, the war highlighted weaknesses of the NATO and EU security system as it pertains to Eastern Europe and specifically to the countries of the former Soviet Union.

DOUGLAS C. LOVELACE, JR.
Director
Strategic Studies Institute

ABOUT THE AUTHORS

ARIEL COHEN is Senior Research Fellow in Russian and Eurasian Studies and International Energy Policy at the Katherine and Shelby Cullom Davis Institute for

International Policy at The Heritage Foundation. He directs conferences on Eurasian security, terrorism and energy, the rule of law, crime and corruption, and a variety of other issues. He also directs Heritage's energy simulation exercises and war games involving Russia (2007-11). Dr. Cohen conducts White House briefings and regularly lectures for the U.S. Government, including the Foreign Service Institute of the U.S. Department of State, the Joint Chiefs of Staff, and the Training and Doctrine and Special Forces Commands of the U.S. armed services, Central Intelligence Agency, and Defense Intelligence Agency. He frequently testifies before committees of the U.S. Congress, including the Senate and House Foreign Relations Committees, House Armed Services Committee, House Judiciary Committee, and the Helsinki Commission. Dr. Cohen is also a Member of the Council on Foreign Relations and International Institute for Strategic Studies (London). Dr. Cohen authored Russian Imperialism: Development and Crisis (Praeger Publishers/Greenwood, 1996 and 1998); edited and co-authored Eurasia in Balance, (Ashgate, United Kingdom, 2005); and authored Kazakhstan: The Road to Independence: Energy Policy and the Birth of a Nation (School of Advanced International Studies, Johns Hopkins Central Asia Caucasus Institute, 2008).

ROBERT E. HAMILTON is a U.S. Army colonel and Eurasian area specialist. His current assignment is as a professor in the Department of National Security and Strategy at the U.S. Army War College. He has served as a strategic war planner and country desk officer at U.S. Central Command, as the Chief of Regional Engagement for Combined Forces CommandAfghanistan, and as the Chief of the Office of Defense Cooperation at the U.S. Embassy in Georgia. Colonel Hamilton was a U.S. Army War College fellow at the Center for Strategic and International Studies in Washington, DC, where he authored several articles about the war between Russia and Georgia and the security situation in the former Soviet Union. Colonel Hamilton is currently completing Ph.D. course work at the University of Virginia.

SUMMARY

Russia launched the war against Georgia in August 2008 for highly valued strategic and geopolitical objectives, which included de facto annexation of Abkhazia, weakening or toppling the Mikheil Saakashvili regime, and preventing North Atlantic Treaty Organization (NATO) enlargement. The Russian politico-military elites had focused on Georgia since the days of the presidency of Eduard Shevardnadze, whom they blamed, together with Soviet president Mikhail Gorbachev and Union of Socialist Soviet Republics (USSR) Communist Party Central Committee Secretary Alexander Yakovlev, for the dissolution of the Soviet empire in Eastern Europe and the dismantlement of the Soviet Union itself.[1]

Russian post-communist security establishments also viewed the attractive Abkhaz coast line and illicit business opportunities provided by lawless Abkhazia and South Ossetia as additional incentives for deep involvement along the metropolitan periphery. Russian military and covert action support of secessionist movements there starting in 1992 should be seen along this continuum. Things only got worse after pro-American, NATO, and European

---

[1] Ronald D. Asmus, *A Little War That Shook the World*, New York: Palgrave-MacMillan, 2010, p. viii.

Union (EU) oriented Mikheil Saakashvili was elected president. Since 2006, the military operation rapidly became the matter of "when," not if.

The war also demonstrated the weaknesses of NATO and the EU security system, because they provided no efficient response to Russia's forced changing of the borders and occupation of an Organization for Security and Cooperation in Europe (OSCE) member state.

The war demonstrated fissures in Europe between the Western powers eager to maintain good relations with Russia, and the Eastern European states which, 20 years after the collapse of the USSR, retain a political memory of the Soviet occupation. Specifically, Germany, France, and Italy were anxious to put the war behind them and treated it as a nuisance, whereas the presidents of Poland, Ukraine, Estonia, and Lithuania and the Prime Minister of Latvia flew to Tbilisi during the war, to stand shoulder to shoulder with Saakashvili.

Despite negative assessments of the Russian military performance both in and outside the Russian Federation, its war goals were mostly achieved and will be analyzed in this monograph. From Russia's geopolitical perspective, the war was a success. The military performance is more difficult to define and evaluate, as this analysis suggests.

Implications of the 2008 Russo-Georgian war for the United States include the following:

- The Vladimir Putin-Dmitry Medvedev administration and the defense establishment formulated far-reaching goals when they carefully prepared over 2 1/2 years for a combined operations-style invasion of Georgia.[2] These goals included effectively terminating Georgian sovereignty in South Ossetia and Abkhazia by solidifying control of the pro-Moscow separatist regimes in Abkhazia and South Ossetia, thus denying Tbilisi control over these territories in perpetuity; expelling Georgian troops and the remaining Georgian population from the two secessionist enclaves; preventing Georgia from joining NATO; sending a strong signal to other post-Soviet states, first and foremost Ukraine, that the pursuit of NATO membership may result in dismemberment and a military invasion.

- In recent years, Moscow granted the majority of the Abkhaz and South Ossetians Russian citizenship. This is a tool of geopolitics that other regimes in Europe practiced in darker eras (1930s in Sudetenland). The use of Russian citizenship to create a "protected" population residing in a neighboring state to undermine its sovereignty is a slippery slope that may lead to a redrawing of the former Soviet borders, including in the Crimea (Ukraine), and possibly in Northern Kazakhstan.

- Russian continental power is on the rise. Small states of Eurasia will treat nuclear armed great powers, such as Russia and China, with respect, especially given the limited American response to the invasion of Georgia (and the current administration's emphasis on the U.S. relationship with Moscow).

- U.S. intelligence-gathering and analysis of the Russian threat to and invasion of Georgia was found lacking. So was U.S. military assistance to Georgia, worth around $2 billion over the last 15 years, since a Russian invasion was not seriously considered to be a strategic threat to the U.S.-friendly country.

---

[2] Ariel Cohen, "Springtime Is for War?" The Heritage Foundation press commentary, originally published by *TechCentralStation* (*TCSDaily*), March 31, 2006, available from *www.heritage.org/Press/Commentary/ed033106a.cfm*.

- International organizations failed to prevent the war and to force Russia to observe the cease-fire conditions.

Among the Russian goals were:

- Bringing down President Saakashvili and installing a more pro-Russian leadership in Tbilisi.
- Providing Russia with control over Abkhazia and South Ossetia, including using their territory and air space for broader defense objectives in the South Caucasus.
- Control of the South Caucasus energy corridor (East-West corridor). If a pro-Russian regime were established in Georgia, it would bring the strategic Baku-Tbilisi-Ceyhan oil pipeline and the Baku-Erzerum (Turkey) gas pipeline under Moscow's control.

RUSSIA'S GEOPOLITICAL GOALS

Moscow formulated far-reaching goals when it carefully prepared—over a period of at least 2 1/2 years, and possibly longer—for a land invasion of Georgia, as Dr. Ariel Cohen warned. These goals included:

- Expelling Georgian troops and effectively terminating Georgian sovereignty in South Ossetia and Abkhazia. Russia prepared the ground for independence and possible eventual annexation of these separatist territories. These goals seem to have been successfully achieved.
- Preventing Georgia from joining the North Atlantic Treaty Organization (NATO) and sending a strong message to Ukraine that its insistence on NATO membership may lead to war and/or its dismemberment. Russia succeeded in attacking a state that, since April 2008, has been regarded as a potential candidate for NATO membership. The Russian assault eroded the effectiveness of the NATO umbrella in Eastern Europe, even though Georgia is not yet formally a member, since it became apparent that Moscow can use force against its neighbors with relative impunity. While it remains to be seen whether Georgia ultimately is accepted into NATO, some voices in Europe (especially in Germany and Italy), saw in the war a vindication of their opposition to such membership. Ukraine's Victor Yushchenko administration stood tall in solidarity with Georgia, and has attempted to take steps to limit the movements of Russia's Black Sea Fleet, but had little domestic support for NATO membership. The Party of Regions effectively sided with Russia during the war, pointing out the disastrous results of Mikheil Saakashvili's NATO enlargement policy for Georgia. The Yanukovich administration, which came to power in early 2010, legislatively enshrined Ukraine's neutrality, including nonmembership in NATO, and granted privileges to the Black Sea Fleet in Sevastopol, Ukraine, until 2042.

Russia's long-term strategic goals included:

- Increasing its control of the Caucasus, especially over strategic energy pipelines. If a pro-Russian regime were established in Georgia, it would have brought the strategic Baku-TbilisiCeyhan oil pipeline and the Baku-Erzurum (Turkey) gas pipeline under Moscow's control. By attempting to accomplish regime change in Georgia, Moscow is also trying to gain control of the energy and transportation corridor that connects Central Asia and Azerbaijan with the Black Sea and ocean routes overseas—for oil, gas, and other commodities. In 1999, Western companies reached an agreement with Central Asian states to create the Baku-Tbilisi-Ceyhan pipeline. So far, this corridor has allowed Azerbaijan and partly Kazakhstan and Turkmenistan, to bypass Russian-controlled pipeline networks and transport its oil from the Caspian Sea basin straight through Georgia and Turkey, without crossing Russian territory.

The growing output of the newly independent Central Asian states has been increasingly competing with Russian oil. By 2018, the Caspian basin, including Kazakhstan and Azerbaijan, is supposed to export up to 4 million barrels of oil a day, as well as a significant amount of natural gas. Russia would clearly like to restore its hegemony over hydrocarbon export routes that would considerably diminish sovereignty and diplomatic freedom of maneuver in these newly independent states.

Russian control over Georgia would outflank Azerbaijan from the West, denying the United States basing and intelligence options there in case of a confrontation with Iran. This kind of control would also undermine any options for pro-Western orientations in Azerbaijan and Armenia, along with any chance of resolving their conflict based on diplomacy and involvement of international organizations. As Russia is strengthening its long-term military presence in Armenia, this scenario seems to be playing out in full.

- Recreating a sphere of influence (a "sphere of privileged interests" in official Russian parlance) in the former Soviet Union and beyond, if/when necessary by use of force. Here, the intended addressees included all former Soviet republics, including the Baltic States. The message may have backfired in the short term, as the presidents of Poland, Ukraine, Estonia, Latvia, and Lithuania came to Tbilisi and stood shoulder-to-shoulder with Saakashvili. However, in the long term, a number of Central and Eastern European states, including Ukraine, Poland, and Lithuania, have improved their relations with Moscow. Without Western European and U.S. support, "New Europe" alone cannot stand up to Moscow. "Regime change" means bringing down President Saakashvili and installing a more pro-Russian leadership in Tbilisi. Russia seems to have given up on the immediate toppling of Saakashvili, and is likely counting on its Georgian political allies to do the job. For a while, Russia talked about pursuing a criminal case against Saakashvili for genocide and war crimes in South Ossetia, to turn him into another Slobodan Milosevic/Radovan Karadzic. This is part of psychological operations against Georgia and its leader.

PRE-CONDITIONS FOR THE WAR

Pro-Russian Separatists Inside Georgia

Russian relations with Georgia were the worst among the post-Soviet states. In addition to fanning the flames of separatism in South Ossetia since 1990, Russia militarily supported separatists in Abkhazia (1992-93), which is also a part of Georgian territory, to undermine Georgia's independence and assert Russia's control over the strategically important South Caucasus.

Despite claims about oppressed minority status, the separatist South Ossetian leaders are mostly ethnic Russians, many of whom served in the Russian Secret Police (KGB); the Russian military; or in the Soviet communist party. Abkhazia and South Ossetia have become Russia's protectorates, their population largely militarized and subsisting on smuggling operations.

This use of small, ethnically- or religiously-based proxies is not unlike Iran's use of Hezbollah and Hamas in the Levant. Tbilisi tried for years to deal with these separatist regimes by offering a negotiated solution, including full autonomy within Georgia. However, the United States and the European Union (EU) members did not pressure Moscow to agree to a settlement. These entreaties were rejected by the separatist regimes in Sukhumi, Abkhazia, and Tskhinvali, South Ossetia, respectively.

In recent years, Moscow granted the majority of Abkhaz and South Ossetians Russian citizenship and moved to establish close economic and bureaucratic ties with the two separatist republics, effectively enacting a creeping annexation of both territories. Use of Russian citizenship to create a "protected" population residing in a neighboring state to undermine its sovereignty is a slippery slope that is leading to a redrawing of the former Soviet borders in Russia's favor.

Georgian attempts to reach out to European capitals and Washington to prevent the war failed. Temur Yakobashvili, Minister in charge of "frozen conflicts," was told not to use the word "war" by an EU bureaucrat on the eve of hostilities, as he was warning that the conflict was imminent.[1] On August 7, 2008, after weeks of Russian-backed South Ossetian military provocation, Saakashvili attacked South Ossetian targets with artillery and armor. Yet, Tbilisi was stunned by the ferocity of the Russian response. It should not have been, nor should the U.S. Government be surprised. The writing was on the wall, but Washington failed to read it, despite repeated warning from allied intelligence services and a massive presence of diplomats and military trainers on the ground.

"Kill the Chicken to Scare the Monkey"

Aggression against Georgia also sends a strong signal to Ukraine and to European states along Russia's borders. Former president and current Prime Minister Vladimir Putin spoke in the spring of 2008 about Russia "dismembering" Ukraine, another NATO candidate, and detaching the Crimea, a peninsula that was transferred from the Russian Federation to Ukraine in 1954 by Soviet leader Nikita Khrushchev, when both were integral parts of the Soviet Union.

Today, up to 50 percent of Ukrainian citizens speak Russian as their first language, and ethnic Russians comprise around one-fifth of Ukraine's population. Yet, Ukraine's pro-Western leaders, such as President Yushchenko and Prime Minister Yulia Timoshenko, have expressed a desire to join NATO, while the pro-Moscow Ukrainian Party of Regions opposes such membership. NATO opponents in Ukraine were greatly encouraged by Russia's action against Georgia. Beyond this, Russia demonstrated that it can sabotage American and EU declarations about integrating the Commonwealth of Independent States (CIS) members into Western structures such as NATO.

Military Performance

The Russian and Georgian performances in the war were in many ways mirror images of each other. Russian strategy was well-thought-out and properly resourced, giving Russia significant advantages at the operational level of war and allowing it to overcome shortcomings at the tactical level. The Georgian military, by contrast, was reasonably well-trained and well-equipped at the small-unit level and fought well in tactical engagements, but the reactive nature of Georgian strategic and operational planning and the often haphazard way in which plans were conceived and implemented undercut the tactical advantages the Georgians enjoyed, thus undermining their entire effort. Indeed, Georgian officers have characterized their operation as "spontaneously" planned, with no reserve designated, no fire support or engineer plans written, and the main effort commander selected only hours before the war began. They have also decried what they describe as significant intervention by the civilian leadership of the country in the minutest details of planning and executing the operation.[2]

In general then, the higher the level of analysis, the more effective the Russian effort appears to have been. At the strategic level, Russia was able to execute a combined political-military strategy that isolated Georgia from its western partners while setting the conditions for military success. At the operational level, these advantages were parlayed into success by the early commitment of a decisive amount of forces to the theater of operations and sufficient, if not especially elegant, operational coordination. At the tactical level, despite disadvantages in capabilities at the small-unit level and use of tactics that exposed its forces to the risk of higher casualties, the offensive-mindedness, superior numbers, and speed of Russian forces committed to the fight overwhelmed their enemy and translated into battlefield victory.

While the Russian armed forces had retained significant elements of their Soviet strategic, operational, and tactical heritage, the Georgian armed forces had jettisoned Soviet doctrine and purged the vast majority of the Soviet-era military leadership. While this meant there was essentially no intellectual resistance to transformation in the Georgian military, it also meant that there was no reservoir of military experience to draw on. Most of Georgia's leadership in the armed forces and the Ministry of Defense was under 40 and had matured professionally in the post-Soviet period. So, a comparison of the Russian and Georgian efforts suggests that—at least in this case—superior strategic and operational planning and execution allowed Russia to overcome tactical disadvantages, while Georgia's tactical advantages were insufficient to overcome the strategic and operational disadvantages it faced, due at least in part to the radical nature of the changes made in senior leadership over the past several years.

MILITARY IMPLICATIONS

The short war fought between Russia and Georgia in August 2008 had implications reaching far beyond the relatively small patch of ground, sea, and air where it was fought. Militarily, the war highlighted both improvements in capabilities and remaining weaknesses on both sides, weaknesses that proved in some cases surprisingly similar, given the radically different training and equipping efforts undertaken by Russia and Georgia in the years prior to the war.

In both countries, the war resulted in far-reaching efforts at reform aimed at addressing these weaknesses. Politically, the war temporarily but seriously undermined the stability of Georgia, exposed latent but deep divisions within NATO on the wisdom of future enlargement, and left Russia temporarily isolated diplomatically, both for its disproportionally violent treatment of Georgia and for its recognition of the self-proclaimed independence by the Georgian secessionist provinces of Abkhazia and South Ossetia. This monograph focuses on the military performance of the Russian armed forces during the war; it examines the defense reform effort that resulted; it reviews and analyzes geopolitical repercussions of the first post-Soviet Russian war beyond its borders; and it draws political and military implications for future NATO and U.S. policy toward Russia and the former Soviet Union.

Forces Deployed

Any assessment of the performance of the Russian armed forces in the war with Georgia must begin with a comparison of Russian and Georgian forces committed to the fight. What is clear is that the war resulted in a military victory for Russia; what is less clear is whether the origin of the victory lies on the strategic, operational, or tactical level, or on some combination of these levels. In other words, was the cause of the Russian victory a superior strategic plan that allowed Russia to use overwhelming force to subdue Georgia; was it superior operational art that consistently maximized Russian firepower and maneuver capabilities while integrating these with other military capabilities; or was it simply greater tactical skill that allowed Russia to consistently win tactical engagements, eventually causing the defeat of the Georgian forces?

One clear fact that emerges from an examination of the forces committed by both sides is that despite significant geographic challenges to the introduction of forces into the theater of combat, Russia managed to assemble, relatively quickly, a force that possessed a significant numerical superiority over its Georgian foe. In South Ossetia, Russia committed the 58th Army, based in the Russian city of Vladikavkaz and consisting of the 19th and 42nd Motorized Rifle Divisions; the 76th Air Assault Division, airlifted to theater from the Russian city of Pskov in the St. Petersburg Military District; and the 98th Airborne Division, to include elements of the 45th Intelligence Regiment, airlifted from their bases near Moscow. A battalion of the 33rd Special Mountain Brigade, a newly formed unit trained and equipped to operate in the challenging terrain of the Caucasus region, was also reportedly deployed to South Ossetia.[3]

Russian military transportation aviation provided the needed support as the forces deployed and engaged in the theater. In all, Russian transport aircraft flew more than 100 sorties to move men, equipment, and supplies to theater before and during the war.[4] Alongside Russian forces fought South Ossetian militias and volunteer forces from the Russian North Caucasus, including the Chechen East and West battalions, dreaded and feared by Georgians due to memories of atrocities they committed during Georgia's civil wars of the 1990s, when they also fought on the side of the Abkhaz separatist forces.

In Abkhazia, where Russia opened a second front on the third day of the war, elements of the 7th Airborne Division from Novorossisk and the 76th Air Assault Division from Pskov landed from the Black Sea alongside naval infantry of the Black Sea Fleet, while elements of the 20th Motorized Division from Volgograd deployed by way of a railroad line from Russia that Russian troops had repaired earlier that year. As in South Ossetia, in Abkhazia Russian forces were augmented by Abkhaz military forces, which were substantially more capable than their South Ossetian counterparts.

Accurate estimates of the total number of Russian and allied forces committed in the war are elusive, but most analysts agree on a figure in the 35,000-40,000 range. Russian military analyst Pavel Felgenhauer estimates that 12,000 Russian troops assisted by "several thousand" South Ossetian and North Caucasus militia fought in South Ossetia, while 15,000 Russian troops fought in Abkhazia. He gives the total number of Russian ground forces deployed as 25,000-30,000, augmented by several thousand militia and deploying some 1,200 armored and self-propelled artillery vehicles, 200 fixed-wing aircraft, and 40 helicopters.[5] American author and former U.S. State Department official Ron Asmus agrees, putting the total number of Russian forces deployed during the course of the war at 40,000.[6]

The Russian air force, while underperforming by Western standards, demonstrated decisive air superiority over its Georgian foe. For the air campaign, Russia assembled a force of some 300 combat aircraft, including the Su-24, Su-25, Su-27, and Tu-22. While one analyst claims they flew 200 total combat sorties over the 5 days of the war,[7] it is likely that the actual figure is higher. Asmus cites a figure of 400 total sorties against 36 targets, with 120 of those sorties flown on the second day of the war alone.[8] Whatever the exact number of sorties flown, what is clear is that Russia enjoyed an overwhelming advantage in aircraft of all types, with some 14 times as many combat aircraft in theater as Georgia.[9]

Moscow committed itself to making the Georgia war a combined forces operation, ordering the Black Sea Fleet into action for the first time since World War II. Russian naval forces arrived in theater late on the second day of the war in the form of Black Sea Fleet ships led by the cruiser *Moskva* and the destroyer *Smetlivy*, along with troop ships and support ships. Given that the distance between their base in Sevastopol and the Georgian Black Sea coast is 400 nautical miles, these ships must have left base immediately upon the outbreak of the war or even before. Their mission was twofold: to land Russian troops in Abkhazia, and to seize and destroy Georgian naval facilities and forces.

Arrayed against the Russian and allied forces were some 12,000-15,000 Georgian troops of the Land Forces Command and the Special Forces Battalion, along with a small number of special police forces. Initially, Georgia committed the 3rd and 4th Infantry Brigades of the Land Forces command to the operation, along with a task force composed primarily of Ministry of Defense and Ministry of the Interior Special Forces units, which together were designated as the main effort. When Georgia's forces in South Ossetia found themselves increasingly outnumbered by their enemy, the Land Forces Command committed the 2nd Infantry Brigade to the fight as well. Georgia's small air force consisted of eight Su-25 attack aircraft and around 25 helicopters, but it played no role in the war after the first day, as the

Georgian leadership decided to ground the air force to preserve it from destruction. Beyond an incident in which the Russian side claimed that four Georgian patrol boats came out of the port of Poti to attack them and were destroyed, the Georgian Navy and Coast Guard had minimal capability and played no role in the war.

Thus, the war between Russia and Georgia saw some 35,000-40,000 Russian and allied forces, augmented by significant air and naval forces, confront some 12,000-15,000 Georgian forces with little air and no naval capability. While it is tempting to assume that any Russia-Georgia war would result in a significant numerical advantage for Russia simply due to the differing sizes of their overall military forces, this view is not necessarily accurate. First, it underestimates the geographical challenges for Russia of rapidly inserting significant numbers of forces into South Ossetia and Abkhazia, the former of which is separated from Russia by the Greater Caucasus mountain range and accessible only by the Roki Tunnel, and the latter of which is most accessible from Russia by sea or by rail. Second, this view minimizes the extent to which Russian preparatory actions were successful in sowing confusion and uncertainty within the Georgian government and preventing any real deterrence of Russian escalation from Georgia's western partners. In short, it was Russia's skillful use and abuse of its mandate and prerogatives as a peacekeeping force in both Abkhazia and South Ossetia that allowed it to set the strategic conditions for success, while preventing its adversary from doing so. And it is to Russian strategy that we now turn.

RUSSIAN PERFORMANCE IN THE WAR

An assessment of Russian performance in the war with Georgia must begin with an overview of Russia's likely objectives for the campaign. A review of Russian military operations in the war; Russian diplomacy before, during, and after the war; and a content analysis of Russian statements about the war lead to the following likely campaign objectives. Primary objectives seem to have been to end Georgia's sovereignty over Abkhazia and South Ossetia permanently, to cripple the Georgian armed forces, and to end Georgia's drive to join NATO. Secondary objectives likely included weakening and possibly toppling the Saakashvili government, exerting a chilling effect on other former Soviet countries considering NATO membership, especially Ukraine, and demonstrating the capability and resolve to end what Russia saw as Western encroachment in its "zone of privileged interests." Finally, it is likely that Russian objectives included an element of revenge for the Western recognition of Kosovo's independence, which Russia had vehemently opposed and vowed to answer.

Strategy

In examining the Russian strategy for the war, it is instructive to begin with an overview of the road to war, since the actions Russia took in the months leading up to August 2008 say much about whether and when Russia expected war and how it hoped to achieve its objectives if war came. Using its military status as the only (in Abkhazia) or the primary (in South Ossetia) peacekeeping force and its political status as a member of the conflict resolution bodies in both provinces, starting in early 2008, Russia undertook a series of political and military tasks designed to sow fear and confusion in the Georgian government, determine whether and how the West would respond to increasing Russian pressure on Georgia, and set the military conditions for success in a war against Georgia. At the same time, as Anton Lavrov wrote in *Tanki Avgusta* (*Tanks of August*), a new, comprehensive Russian book about the conflict, "it became clear [to the Russian leadership] that the only means to defend these unrecognized republics was direct military intervention of the Russian army in case of Georgia's attempt to return separatist republics by force."[10]

Politically, Russia identified and skillfully exploited the gap between Georgian and Western policies with respect to the "frozen conflicts" of Abkhazia and South Ossetia. In early 2008, Russia began to ratchet up the political and diplomatic pressure on Tbilisi. On March 6, then-President Putin announced that Russia was unilaterally withdrawing from the sanctions regime imposed by the CIS that prohibited the delivery of military equipment to Abkhazia. On April 16, the Russian government announced that it was establishing direct government-to-government contact with the unofficial governments in Abkhazia and South Ossetia, a step that Georgia claimed amounted to *de facto* recognition of those regimes.

As Russian pressure increased, Georgia repeatedly called for internationalization and civilianization of the peacekeeping forces in Abkhazia and South Ossetia, arguing that Russia had become a party to the conflict and therefore was unsuited to its role as lead nation in the peacekeeping forces. Western governments and international organizations took notice and embarked on renewed efforts to move the peace process forward. The German government, the EU, and the Organization for Security and Cooperation in Europe (OSCE) all put forth revised peace plans or sponsored peace conferences. The German peace plan for Abkhazia was accepted by Georgia but rejected by the Abkhaz *de facto* government; Russia and the separatist governments failed to appear at an EU-sponsored peace conference on Abkhazia and rejected an OSCE suggestion for renewed negotiations on South Ossetia.[11]

This combination of political pressure and blocked attempts to restart the process of negotiations caused Georgia to become more insistent in its warnings that what was underway was a *de facto* Russian annexation of Abkhazia and South Ossetia. In response, Georgia's Western partners attempted to reassure Tbilisi of their commitment to its Euro-Atlantic aspirations, while warning the government not to allow itself to be provoked by Russia into a war that it could not hope to win. The Georgian response was that it had red lines in Abkhazia and South Ossetia that—if crossed— would require a response.[12] Other former Soviet countries, especially Ukraine and the Baltic Republics, tended to sympathize with Georgia's plight and tried to echo Georgian concerns to Western governments. As early as March 2008, as least one of the intelligence services of the Baltic Republics was warning that Russia planned a war against Georgia later that year and that the 58th Army and the 76th Air Assault Division would participate.[13] But these warnings were not communicated often enough and at a high enough level to attract significant Western attention.

In essence, the West and Georgia were talking past each other, with the former taking the long view toward Georgia's eventual NATO membership and cautioning it not to do anything in the short term to damage that process, and the latter insisting that its sovereignty and territorial integrity were being compromised and warning that it could not stand by while Russia continued a process that amounted to annexation of Georgian territory. Apparently forgotten by the West in its desire to at once reassure and restrain Georgia was any meaningful attempt to deter Russia from further destabilizing actions. By the eve of the war, then, Russia could be relatively certain that it had succeeded in unnerving the Georgian government to the point that its decisionmaking processes—never especially coherent to begin with—were significantly compromised, and that it had also identified a gap between Western and Georgian policies toward the frozen conflicts that could be exploited to good effect.

Russian military actions in this period were bold and well-coordinated with Russian political moves. C. W. Blandy has remarked that "traditionally the Russian military mind, as embodied in the general staff, looks farther ahead than its Western counterpart, on the basis that 'foresight implies control'."[14] Working backward from their military objectives, the Russian armed forces began a series of military tasks that were dual use in nature—while they could conceivably (sometimes barely conceivably) be characterized as legitimate under Russia's peacekeeping mandate, they also served as preparatory tasks for an invasion of Georgia by probing Georgian defenses, introducing new Russian forces to theater, or repairing infrastructure required for offensive operations.

As with its political counterpart, the Russian military escalation began in Abkhazia. On April 20, a Russian aircraft intercepted and shot down a Georgian unmanned aerial vehicle (UAV) over Abkhazia. Despite Russian denials, an international group of experts pinned the blame for this incident on Russia, in part due to the fact that the UAV was able to capture and transmit images of its killer—a Russian fighter with the tricolor tail flash plainly visible—just before its demise. Later in April, Russia deployed an additional 500 troops to Abkhazia, which it was authorized to do under the peacekeeping agreement, but this also succeeded in raising the level of tension in Tbilisi, as the Georgian government saw both the timing of the deployment and the type of unit deployed—an airborne battalion—as evidence that Russia was again raising the stakes of the confrontation. Finally, in late May, Russia announced that it was deploying railroad troops to repair a key railroad line in Abkhazia. This was a signal that the war was imminent. When Georgia protested that these troops were in fact illegal under the peacekeeping agreement, Russia responded by characterizing their mission as humanitarian. During the war, this railroad line was used to move Russian troops and supplies through Abkhazia. Finally, the Georgians claimed that their sources had observed 26 shipping containers of military equipment enter Abkhazia in the spring of 2008, including D30 howitzers, SA11 and ZSU 23-4 air defense systems, and BM21 multiple launch rocket systems.[15]

It is possible that Russia expected a more robust Georgian response to its moves in Abkhazia than it received. Although the Georgian armed forces did deploy key military leadership and enablers (especially aviation assets) to western Georgia to set up a command post there in April-May 2008, and it did put its ground units on a higher state of alert, the Georgian government was careful not to take any actions that might give Russia a pretext for war. The George W. Bush administration warned Tbilisi at the highest level not to provoke the Russians.[16]

The nature of the peacekeeping forces and the demographic makeup of Abkhazia might also have played a role. In Abkhazia the peacekeeping force deployed under the auspices of the CIS was entirely Russian, whereas in South Ossetia the peacekeeping forces had Georgian, Russian, and South Ossetian contingents, providing troublemakers on both sides with ample targets if they wished to precipitate a crisis.

Additionally, in Abkhazia there were only two regions where appreciable numbers of ethnic Georgians remained—the Gali district in the far southeastern corner of the province and the Kodori Gorge in the far northeastern corner. The result of this was that the Georgian and Abkhaz populations in Abkhazia were more separated from one another than were the Georgian and Ossete populations in South Ossetia, where Georgian and Ossete villages were intermingled. This intermingling of populations in South Ossetia provided permissive conditions for the descent into violence in early-August 2008.

In any case, after escalation in Abkhazia failed to provoke a crisis, Russian attention seemed to shift to South Ossetia. Blandy says that as early as May 2008, units from the Russian 58th Army began setting up assembly areas along the length of the highway from the army's garrison in Vladikavkaz to the Roki Tunnel, the only road avenue of approach into South Ossetia.[17] While these assembly areas could conceivably have been related to preparations for the Russian exercise *Kavkaz* (Caucasus) '08, which began in mid-July, the exercise itself can be seen as a preparatory task for the invasion of Georgia. Although the official scenario for the exercise was a counterterrorist operation, the operational and tactical scenarios involved an intervention in a fictional neighboring country.[18] Exercise participants received a card reading, "Soldier, Know Your Probable Enemy!" On the card were listed key personnel and equipment data on the Georgian Armed Forces, along with their assessed strengths and weaknesses. This was another signal that war was imminent.

Inside South Ossetia and in the airspace over it, Russian and allied forces escalated the situation and put themselves at an operational and tactical advantage if and when war came. On July 8, the same day that U.S. Secretary of State Condoleezza Rice was visiting Tbilisi, four Russian Su-24s flew over the international border and loitered over South Ossetia for some 40 minutes, eliciting a strong protest from Tbilisi. This air incursion, which Russia acknowledged openly, was likely meant to send a signal of Russian capability and resolve and also perhaps to test Georgian and U.S. responses.

In fact, Russian air incursions into Georgia had been ongoing for over a year prior to the outbreak of war. In March 2007, Mi24 helicopters attacked Georgian government buildings in the Kodori Gorge, the only portion of Abkhazia then under Georgian government control. Then, in August 2007, an aircraft launched a Kh-58 missile at a Georgian air defense radar site, but the missile missed its target and failed to explode, providing the Georgian government with strong evidence of Russian responsibility for the attack. In both cases, Georgia turned physical evidence from the attack sites along with radar-tracking data over to teams of international experts, who concluded that only Russia could have launched the strikes. The intent of these attacks was likely threefold—to raise the level of military pressure on Georgia, to damage or to destroy Georgian military and government infrastructure, and to assess Georgian capabilities to respond.

Finally, Russia apparently infiltrated the advance elements of the units designated to take part in the war into South Ossetia in the days immediately prior to the outbreak of the hostilities. For instance, multiple reports in the Russian press (some of which were later retracted) and from Georgian intelligence sources indicated that the advance elements of the 135th and 693rd Motorized Rifle Regiments entered South Ossetia on or before August 7.[19] Indeed, Abkhaz President Sergei Bagapsh announced as much when he indicated on Abkhaz television on August 7 that a battalion from Russia's North Caucasus Military district had entered South Ossetia and stabilized the situation there.[20] It is also likely that volunteer forces—most likely elements of the Chechen East and West battalions—from the Russian North Caucasus entered South Ossetia prior to the initiation of hostilities. Among multiple reports of their presence is the statement by head of the South Ossetian Security Council

Anatoly Barankevich on the morning of August 7 that South Ossetia had requested assistance from the Russian province of North Ossetia, and that armed groups from there were on their way.[21]

So by the late-evening hour of 11:35 p.m. of August 7, just hours away from the start of the war (usually pegged to the Georgian artillery bombardment of targets in and around the South Ossetian capital of Tskhinvali), a combined and integrated Russian political and military strategy had delivered several key successes. First, it had succeeded in degrading the quality of Georgian political and military decisionmaking by raising and sustaining the pressure on Georgia's political and military leadership. Second, it had succeeded in identifying and exploiting a gap between Georgian and Western policies that eventually led Georgia to conclude that it had no choice but to fight a war it had little chance of winning, and to fight that war alone. And finally, the policy had succeeded in changing the military balance in both Abkhazia and South Ossetia in ways that were favorable to itself and its allies without taking any steps that the West would conclusively see as an initiation of hostilities.

Timing of the Hostilities Outbreak. While in hindsight it seems obvious that Russia was determined to fight if war came, that fact was not obvious to Georgian decisionmakers at the time. Despite the increase in tensions with Russia, the Georgian leadership expected a repeat of previous skirmishes in South Ossetia, in which the Georgian army would confront South Ossetian militias backed by volunteer forces from the Russian North Caucasus and only limited artillery and aviation support from the Russian armed forces. Georgian Chief of the Joint Staff Brigadier General Zaza Gogava later told a parliamentary commission of inquiry into the war that Georgian intelligence "was not comprehensive enough to indicate that such a large-scale Russian military intervention was to be expected."[22] The reasons for this failure are several— Georgia's poor intelligence picture, the degradation in Georgian decisionmaking capabilities brought on by sustained Russian pressure, the fact that low-level violence is endemic during the July-August "shooting season" in South Ossetia, and probably plain wishful thinking—but the consequences for the Georgian armed forces were dire. Poor Georgian planning and an early breakdown of Georgian command and control once the operation began compounded these effects.[23]

If the Georgian leadership misread the Russian determination to fight, Russian decisionmakers—having set the strategic conditions for success in the upcoming war— seemed to have been caught off guard by the timing of its outbreak. When war came during the night of August 7-8, Russian Prime Minister Vladimir Putin, largely seen as the architect of the Russian political strategy, was at the opening ceremonies of the Beijing Olympics. On the military side, Chief of the General Staff General Nikolai Makarov was newly appointed, while the Chief of the Main Operations Directorate had been dismissed and no replacement yet been named.[24] Finally, the Russian General Staff was in the process of moving into a new building on August 7, meaning its ability to coordinate operations and communicate securely were temporarily degraded.

So despite several months of escalation designed to precipitate a crisis in Georgia, the Russian leadership was initially off balance when the war began, but was able to quickly adjust to the situation. Prime Minister Putin flew from Beijing to 58th Army headquarters in Vladikavkaz, met with key military leaders, and likely issued final guidance on political and possibly military objectives for the campaign. Several Georgian officials have noted that Putin's arrival in Vladikavkaz corresponded with a significant intensification of Russian air and artillery attacks and the expansion of the war to Abkhazia.

There is also a Georgian narrative—not entirely unconvincing—that the Russian plan was for the war to begin later in August, and that the Georgian move on Tskhinvali preempted it. Whatever the case, the outbreak of the war was precipitated by a months-long series of Russian strategic moves that deftly set the conditions for political and military success in the campaign.

Operations

Having set the conditions for success on the strategic level, Russia now had to undertake offensive operations to translate this to success on the battlefield. The introduction of volunteer forces from the North Caucasus Republics and the lead elements of the 135th and 693rd Motorized Rifle Regiments into South Ossetia prior to the outbreak of the war allowed Russia and its South Ossetian allies to prevent Georgia from fully achieving its objectives of securing the critical road junctions north of Tskhinvali and blocking the exit of the Roki Tunnel to prevent the deployment of additional Russian forces. Georgian forces did move through Tskhinvali and had a meeting engagement with Russian forces, probably the advance elements of the 135th and 693rd Regiments, north of the town.

Although the tactical outcome of this first meeting engagement between Georgian and Russian forces was inconclusive, the presence of Russian forces that far south in significant strength caused the Georgian Land Forces Command to adjust its plan. The Georgian plan originally called for the main body of friendly forces to move quickly through Tskhinvali and seize the key road junctions and villages to the north of the city. The engagement with Russian forces there in significant numbers forced the Georgians to commit first one, then two, and finally all three infantry battalions of the 4th Brigade in support of the main effort in and north of Tskhinvali. This left a gap in the west of the Georgian zone of operations, which was eventually filled by the deployment of the 2nd Brigade, initially held in reserve at its base in Senaki in western Georgia. The need for Georgia to commit the 4th Brigade to the main effort and backfill it with the 2nd Brigade had two adverse effects for the Georgian effort. First, the change in mission for the 4th Brigade temporarily left a critical road unguarded. This road leads northwest out of Tskhinvali through the towns of Dzari and Didi Gupta to the town of Java, where Russia had upgraded its refueling facility a year earlier. Leaving it unguarded meant that Russian forces moving south from Java could reach the northern outskirts of Tskhinvali unmolested, and Russia took advantage of this Georgian error. Russian analyst Mikhail Barabanov says that by the afternoon of August 8, the 135th, 693rd, and 503rd Motorized Rifle Regiments of the 19th Motorized Rifle Division had moved south from Java along this road all the way to the northwestern edge of Tskhinvali,[25] where they engaged in pitched battles with Georgian forces. The second consequence of the commitment of the Georgian 4th Brigade to the main effort and its backfill by the 2nd Brigade would not be felt until days later. The commitment of the 2nd Brigade to South Ossetia left western Georgia essentially undefended, and Russia would exploit this situation when the forces it committed in Abkhazia rolled into western Georgia on August 11 and destroyed critical military infrastructure there, most notably the 2nd Brigade base in the town of Senaki and the Georgian Naval base in Poti.

The first significant Georgian defeat came in the opening stages of the war. Georgia was unable to secure or block the exit of the Roki Tunnel—the only route into South Ossetia from

Russia—primarily due to the fact that Georgian artillery lacked the range and accuracy to hit the tunnel's exit, and the fact that Russian forces had secured the tunnel's exit and deployed advance forces through it prior to the outbreak of the war. Georgia was therefore reduced to attempting to interdict the movement of Russian forces south through the use of air attacks (the Georgian air force did not fly after August 8) and cluster munitions fired from BM21 rocket launchers. There is evidence that this did slow the movement of Russian forces south temporarily by damaging the bridge at the town of Gupta,[26] but once the road and bridge had been cleared and repaired, the inexorable movement of Russian forces through the tunnel and down the road to Tskhinvali resumed. Barabanov says that by August 10, in addition to the three regiments from the 19th Motorized Rifle Division committed earlier, Russia had deployed the following forces to South Ossetia: the 70th and 71st Motorized Rifle Regiments of the 42nd Motorized Rifle Division; elements of the 104th and 234th Airborne Regiments from the 76th Air Assault Division; elements of the 45th Intelligence Regiment; and elements of the 10th and 22nd Special Forces Brigades, as well as significant armor, artillery and air defense formations. By this time, Russia had opened a second front in Abkhazia by deploying units from the 7th Airborne and 76th Air Assault Divisions, the 20th Motorized Rifle Division, and two battalions of Naval Infantry from the Black Sea Fleet.[27]

So the strategic preparation for war allowed Russia to begin it on advantageous terms—even though the timing of the war's outbreak seems to have come as a surprise to the Russian political and military leadership—and the rapid introduction of significant forces into the theater of operations allowed Russia to translate strategic preparation into operational advantage. Subsequent sections of this monograph will assess Russian efforts to conduct joint operations, but it is worth noting here some operational lessons learned about the performance of Russian ground forces. Russian military assessments have generally concluded that Russian ground forces were the most effective and best-performing element of the overall Russian effort.[28] However, there are two qualifiers to this assessment. First, as mentioned previously, the Russian success in setting the strategic conditions for war allowed their ground forces to enjoy advantageous force ratios vis-à-vis Georgian forces from very early in the war. Second, it does not appear that all ground forces performed equally well. At least one analyst has claimed that due to the uneven quality of the motorized rifle units committed to the fight, Russian airborne and Special Forces units bore the brunt of the fighting in the war against Georgia.[29]

Coordination between Russian maneuver forces and supporting artillery was generally assessed as good, although some observers have argued that there were relatively few direct fire engagements between large Russian and Georgian maneuver units.[30] If true, this would mean that the apparent Russian success in integrating maneuver and fire support may be less due to Russian operational skill and more to the fact that there were few cases in which artillery had to be used in support of forces in contact with the enemy. Other sources have remarked that Russian use of massive force and coordination with irregular forces was particularly effective.[31] Having trained the North Caucasus volunteer forces, the Russian military was aware of their strengths and weaknesses and used them in roles that maximized the former and minimized the latter. In summary, then, successful preparation for war on the strategic level translated into a significant advantage for Russian forces on the operational level. Russia exploited this advantage by committing a significantly greater number of forces to the fight than Georgia was able to; by using its better-trained units in key roles; by adequate coordination between units, including artillery; by relying on typical Soviet doctrinal tenets of operational speed and overwhelming concentrations of forces at key points; and by making good use of irregular forces to complement the efforts of its conventional forces. All in all, it was an impressive 21st century engagement against a smaller, weaker enemy, adequate for achievement of Moscow's geopolitical goals.

Tactics

Russian strategic and operational advantages were such that victory in the war against Georgia did not depend to any great degree on Russian tactical skill. Indeed, at the tactical level, in direct fire engagements between Russian and Georgian units of relatively equal size, Georgian forces seem to have inflicted more damage than they suffered. In part, this was due to superior Georgian equipment—many Georgian tanks and infantry fighting vehicles were equipped with reactive armor, night vision equipment, advanced radios, and superior fire control systems installed under contract by an Israeli defense firm, while most Russian vehicles lacked these improvements. Georgian forces also benefited from training administered by U.S. and other Western countries designed to prepare them for their deployments to Kosovo and Iraq. While generally focused on stability operations or counterinsurgency, this training taught skills relevant to conventional engagements at the tactical level as well—skills such as reacting to contact and using firepower to support maneuver against the enemy.

Russian forces, in contrast, generally used Soviet tactics, moving in column formation, fighting from the lead elements and continuing to press forward after making contact. They generally made no attempt to stop, establish support by fire positions, and maneuver to the flanks of the Georgian units they encountered.[32] These tactics, employed as they were against a Western-trained force, nearly had disastrous consequences for the Russian effort when the command group of the 58th Army, including the commander, General Anatoly Khruliev, was almost completely destroyed by Georgian forces. Of the 30 vehicles in the command group, 25 were destroyed, killing a significant number of officers and soldiers, and wounding the Army Commander.[33] In another engagement, Georgian reconnaissance units identified a convoy of Russian armor and mechanized forces descending a mountain road northwest of Tskhinvali on the evening of August 9. When Georgian tanks engaged this column, the Russian vehicles appeared confused, failing to return fire and acting as if they were coming under artillery fire.[34]

Despite the high risk entailed by the use of Soviet tactics in the war against Georgia, they did provide a number of advantages to Russian units. The first of these was speed. Declining to deploy upon contact, using support by fire positions, and maneuvering to the flank of enemy units allowed Russian forces—at the cost of higher casualties—to continue to press their advance southward through South Ossetia and into Georgia proper. This kept up the pressure on Georgian forces and certainly had an advantageous psychological effect, since as noted earlier the Georgian military did not believe Russia would fight for South Ossetia on such a significant scale. The second advantage to the use of Soviet tactics lies in their simplicity. For units in which vehicles are not equipped with navigation systems, night vision systems, advanced radios, and advanced fire control systems, the use of tight column formations with the lead elements fighting and the rest of the formation pushing through contact might be the best way to maintain unit integrity and sustain the advance. Finally,

Russian maneuver tactics—especially combined as they were with massive air and artillery attacks against Georgian forces—seem to have had a significant shock effect on Georgian forces, as testified to by the significant number of Georgian vehicles left abandoned on the battlefield.

In general, then, the higher the level of analysis, the more effective the Russian effort appears to have been. At the strategic level Russia was able to execute a combined political-military strategy that isolated Georgia from its Western partners while setting the conditions for military success. At the operational level, these advantages were parlayed into success by the early commitment of a decisive amount of forces to the theater of operations and sufficient, if not especially elegant, operational coordination. At the tactical level, despite disadvantages in capabilities at the small-unit level and use of tactics that exposed its forces to the risk of higher casualties, the offensive-mindedness, superior numbers, and speed of Russian forces committed to the fight overwhelmed their enemy and translated into battlefield victory.

Interestingly, the Russian and Georgian performances in the war were in many ways mirror images of each other. Russian strategy was well-thought-out and properly resourced, giving Russia significant advantages at the operational level of war and allowing it to overcome shortcomings at the tactical level. The Georgian military, by contrast, was reasonably well-trained and well-equipped at the small-unit level and fought well in tactical engagements, but the reactive nature of Georgian strategic and operational planning and the often haphazard way in which plans were conceived and implemented undercut the tactical advantages the Georgians enjoyed and undermined their entire effort. Indeed, Georgian officers have characterized their operation as spontaneously planned, with no reserve designated, no fire support or engineer plans written, and the main-effort commander selected only hours before the war began. They have also decried what they describe as significant intervention by the civilian leadership of the country in the minutest details of planning and executing the operation.[35]

While the Russian armed forces had retained significant elements of their Soviet strategic, operational, and tactical heritage, the Georgian armed forces had jettisoned Soviet doctrine and purged the vast majority of the Soviet-era military leadership. While this meant there was essentially no intellectual resistance to transformation in the Georgian military, it also meant that there was no reservoir of military experience to draw on. Most of Georgia's leadership in the armed forces and the Ministry of Defense were under 40 and had matured professionally in the post-Soviet period. A comparison of the Russian and Georgian efforts thus suggests that—at least in this case—superior strategic and operational planning and execution allowed Russia to overcome tactical disadvantages, while Georgia's tactical advantages were insufficient to overcome the strategic and operational disadvantages it suffered, due at least in part to the radical nature of the changes made in senior leadership over the past several years.

Personnel

Assessments of the effectiveness of the Russian personnel system in the war have highlighted two key deficiencies. The first of these is the lack of adequate numbers of professional soldiers (*kontraktniky*), a deficiency that forced Russian commanders to deploy conscripts despite an official policy banning their use in wars.[36] Russian news media reports indicated that only 70 percent of the soldiers who fought in the war against Georgia were *kontraktniky,* the rest were conscripts.[37] Aside from the fact that the use of conscripts in war violates Russian Ministry of Defense policy—a fact that is of limited relevance to Western analysis— the problem with the deployment of conscripts is their generally low level of training for war. In a war against a more substantial foe this deficiency might have extremely negative effects on Russian performance.

A second problem with the personnel system exposed by the war was the failure of the system of cadre units within the Russian military. Chief of the General Staff Makarov told journalists in December 2008 that "less than 20% of our units are battle-ready, while the rest have only officers without privates."[38] While the existence of these cadre units has long been a fact within the Russian armed forces—their purpose being to allow Russia to rapidly expand its armed forces in case of major war—their existence and their role in the war against Georgia point to a structural problem for the Russian military. First, the fact that personnel from cadre units had to be deployed in the war highlights the fact that even Russia's first-line units are not prepared to go to war "as is," without outside augmentation. Second, when the Russian military leadership called on the staffs of these cadre units to serve in Georgia, they were apparently shocked by how incompetent many of them were. Makarov says, "We were forced to handpick colonels and generals from all over Russia"[39] to replace the ineffective commanders of cadre units. Both of these problems—the role of conscripts and the status of cadre units—are significant areas of emphasis in Russia's current military reform effort.

Equipment and Weapons Systems

We have seen that in many cases Georgian forces were better equipped than their Russian counterparts. Margarete Klein estimated that some 80 percent of Russian weaponry had not been refurbished since the collapse of the Soviet Union in 1991.[40] The effects of this are felt in reduced capability as well as maintenance problems, both of which were in evidence among Russian equipment in the war. It has also been noted that Georgian tanks and infantry fighting vehicles were generally better equipped than were their Russian counterparts, but this comparison held for other equipment as well. Most Georgian Su-25s had been upgraded by the same Israeli firm that upgraded Georgia's tanks; the result was that Georgian aircraft tended to have superior communication, avionics, and weapon-control systems than did Russian aircraft. Even on the individual soldier level, the comparison held, as Georgian soldiers were equipped with advanced helmets and body armor that Russian soldiers lacked. There are a number of reports of Russian soldiers stripping the helmets and body armor from dead Georgians in order to improve their personal protection. Russian forces apparently failed to use even the protective equipment they had. At least one analyst writes that Russian tanks and infantry carriers were subject to destruction by Georgian rocket-propelled grenades (RPGs) because they failed to fill their reactive armor canisters before they deployed.[41] By contrast, a senior Georgian official claims that RPGs were ineffective against Georgian armored vehicles, which deployed with their reactive armor canisters filled.[42]

In addition to reduced combat capability, the failure to upgrade or refurbish Russian equipment since the end of the Soviet Union made it felt in the significant maintenance problems experienced by Russian forces. There are reports of scores of broken Russian vehicles lining the road to South Ossetia, impeding the movement of follow-on forces.[43] This fact, combined with the flow of civilians fleeing the fighting, jammed the single road into South Ossetia and hampered the movement of Russian equipment into the area of operations.[44] Indeed, the Russian maintenance problem was evident even to the Georgians, with a senior Georgian official claiming that over the course of the war, 60-70 percent of Russian tanks and armored vehicles broke down.[45]

Russian equipment deficiencies were not limited to the maneuver forces. Russian military officers, and both Russian and foreign analysts, have noted the lack of counterbattery radars, lack of access to satellite imagery for intelligence planning, lack of electronic warfare capability, and a shortage of unmanned aerial vehicles as well as the poor quality of those available as factors that significantly degraded the Russian effort.[46] The lack of reliable UAVs and satellite imagery is what apparently led the Russian air force to send a Tu-22 bomber deep into Georgia on a reconnaissance and targeting mission, where it was shot down by Georgian air defenses.[47] Within the air force, two related deficiencies stand out. The first is the fact that GLONASS, the Russian answer to the U.S. Global Positioning System (GPS), had not been completed in time for the war. This, combined with the fact that GPS data for Georgia were interrupted during the war, made the use of GPS or GLONASS guided precision munitions impossible. The second problem was the overall lack of precision-guided munitions (PGMs), meaning that even munitions with other guidance systems (laser, for example) were not available in sufficient numbers. These deficiencies led to a significant degradation of the Russian air force's ability to identify and engage important targets, the details of which will be discussed later.

JOINT OPERATIONS:
AN ASSESSMENT OF OPERATIONAL COORDINATION

The war against Georgia represents possibly the first case in which Russian ground, air, and naval components fought together in significant numbers since the end of World War II. Most analyses of the performance of these components give the ground component passing marks but note several deficiencies, give the naval component high marks but admit that it faced no serious opposition, and reserve their harshest criticism for the air component. As far as the coordination among them is concerned, most analyses describe it as coordination in timing of operations only; in other words, Russian operations were coincident in time but can be characterized as joint on only the most superficial level.[48] There did not appear to be unity of command in the joint sense, either. For instance, the commander of the North Caucasus Military District, the nominal overall commander, is said to have had no control over the air force aircraft operating in his theater. Instead, air force operations were personally directed by Commander of the Air Force Colonel-General Aleksander Zelin, who controlled his forces via mobile phone from his office in Moscow.[49]

Ground Forces

Russian armored and mechanized forces in our discussion of Russian operations and tactics have already been assessed. To reiterate, Russian maneuver forces were hampered by serious maintenance issues that combined with the existence of a single axis of advance to hamper the deployment of follow-on forces. Despite this, Russia's introduction into South Ossetia of advance guard forces and North Caucasus volunteer forces prior to the start of the war meant that Russia and its allies enjoyed a numerical advantage almost from the start of combat operations, and this advantage grew as follow-on forces pushed past broken vehicles and fleeing civilians into South Ossetia once the war began. Russian maneuver was unimaginative and caused higher casualties than necessary, but served to keep pressure on Georgian forces and had the advantage of simplicity. Coordination between Russian maneuver forces and artillery was generally assessed as good.[50] Additionally, the war with Georgia represents the first use of the Iskander-M tactical ballistic missile system, which was universally praised for its accuracy and effectiveness.[51]

Russian air assault and airborne forces are assessed to have fought well. However, they were generally used in a standard infantry role rather than being inserted in key areas of the battlefield via airborne or air assault operations. Among the airborne forces, the 76th Air Assault Division has been singled out for praise by Russian observers.[52] There are two possible reasons that these forces were used in a standard infantry role. The first is lack of confidence among the Russian military leadership in the capabilities of the conventional motorized rifle units deployed to Georgia; the second is the fact that the Russian air force was resistant to using helicopters for air assault operations because it was focused on the fixed-wing air campaign and because it considered the air defense threat too high.[53] If the latter is the case, this speaks not only to a lack of joint coordination between the army and the air force but also to a lack of an overall joint commander.

Air Forces

Both Russian and foreign analysts have criticized the performance of the Russian air force in the war against Georgia. The war exposed significant weaknesses in several key capabilities—especially suppression of enemy air defenses (SEAD), reconnaissance and targeting, and strategic attack. In addition, Russian aircraft lacked the ability to operate at night, had very little electronic-warfare capability, and made sparing use of precision-guided missiles (PGMs).[54] Carolina Vendel and Frederik Westerlund state that the Russian air component demonstrated a "remarkably limited capacity to wage air combat for a country aspiring to be a military great power."[55]

Russian tactical aviation assets in their close air support (CAS) role were also criticized for providing little to no support to Russian ground forces in contact with the enemy.[56] Poor coordination between Russian ground and air forces certainly played a role in this; Vendel and Westerlund say that the lack of interoperable radios between army and air force units and the lack of forward air controllers severely limited the extent to which the air force could support ground units in contact.[57] It is also likely that the Georgian air defense threat, which proved much more robust than expected, contributed to this deficiency. Russian air interdiction (AI) appeared to have been more effective, with multiple Georgian officials, chief among them the Chief of the Joint Staff Gogava, having indicated that a significant portion of Georgian combat losses in and around Tskhinvali came from Russian aircraft.[58]

The Russian strategic attack plan executed by long-range aircraft suffered from a lack of good intelligence on potential targets, a higher than expected Georgian air defense threat, and a lack of PGMs. The result was a poorly planned and executed strategic attack effort that bombed military infrastructure of no importance while neglecting important military infrastructure and resulted in high levels of collateral damage (for which the Russian high command may have not cared). For instance, Russian aircraft bombed the airfields at Vaziani near Tbilisi and Kopitnari, west of Kutaisi, neither of which has been used for military flights since the collapse of the Soviet Union. While bombing these unimportant targets, Russian aircraft completely neglected to attack the new Georgian military bases at Gori and Khoni, both of which were of considerable importance. The base at Gori was eventually damaged, but only after Russian ground forces rolled into it and began to dismantle and destroy military infrastructure and capture idle military vehicles.

This poor targeting effort is almost inexplicable when one considers that the Georgian government had been eager to show off its new bases and had taken several groups of foreign military and diplomatic personnel to them after they opened. Furthermore, the new base in Gori sits astride the main Georgian east-west highway, meaning it would have been visible to Russian Embassy personnel as they traveled within Georgia in the course of their normal duties. Given the poor intelligence picture, what appears to have happened is that instead of constructing a coherent and comprehensive targeting plan for the war against Georgia, the leadership of the Russian air force relied on old Soviet maps and data to determine which military targets to attack. There are even indications that the pilot of the Tu-22 shot down by Georgian air defenses was transferred from an academic assignment to a combat flying assignment upon the outbreak of the war because he had been stationed in Georgia during the Soviet period and knew where Georgian airfields were located.[59]

There were also several instances in which Russian aircraft attacked civilian targets, such as apartment buildings, schools, and hospitals. Since these have no military value as targets and since attacking them resulted in significant public relations problems for the Russian military, it is highly unlikely that they were deliberately attacked. A more likely scenario is that the lack of PGMs, the high air defense threat, and the poor intelligence picture constructed by Russian targeters caused pilots either to accidentally attack civilian infrastructure that had been misidentified as military, or to release their bombs at the wrong time or place due to an understandable reluctance to fly low and slow enough to attack the proper target with the dumb bombs available to them.

As implied above, the most significant failure in the Russian air campaign was in the SEAD. The generally accepted figure for Russian aircraft losses is 7-8, with one of these having been a case of fratricide.[60] At least part of the blame for the poor SEAD effort must be laid at the feet of the Russian intelligence community. The Russian air force was unaware that Georgia had purchased the BUK M1 (SA11) anti-aircraft missile system from Ukraine prior to the outbreak of the war, even though Georgia had publicly reported this purchase. This system accounted for a significant portion of the Russian aircraft losses during the war.[61] Russia also appeared to have been unaware that Georgia had purchased the Rafael Spyder anti-aircraft system from Israel, although this was also public knowledge.

However, even had the Russian military leadership known the true extent of Georgia's air defense capability, this might not have prevented the loss of Russian aircraft. Tor Bukvoll claims that Russia made no use of anti-radiation missiles during the air campaign against Georgia. This is likely attributable to two factors. The first is that Georgian air defense units generally kept their radars off until they knew they had Russian aircraft in range, at which time they turned their radars on only long enough to acquire the target and fire at it.[62] The second reason is that Russia may have had little confidence in the capabilities of its anti-radiation missiles to destroy Georgian radars, given the failure of the Russian Kh-58 anti-radiation missile in the August 2007 attack on the Georgian radar near the town of Tsitelubani. In summary, a poor intelligence effort, effective Georgian tactics, and lack of reliable equipment crippled the Russian SEAD effort, and this had deleterious effects for the entire Russian air campaign.

The only air force assets that avoided significant criticism of their performance in the war were transport aviation, both fixed-wing and rotary-wing. As mentioned previously, fixed-wing transport aircraft flew more than 100 sorties to bring soldiers and equipment to theater before and immediately after the outbreak of the war.[63] Units from as far away as Moscow and St. Petersburg were airlifted to the theater on short notice, although all of them, including airborne units, were landed at friendly airfields instead of making combat jumps.[64] Once in theater, airborne and air assault units fought in a standard infantry role. Their use in an airmobile or air assault role was restricted by the air defense threat and the fact that the Russian air force controlled the transport helicopter fleet and was unwilling to use it in support of ground operations. This has led some of the Russian army leadership to argue that some or all of the transport helicopter fleet should be transferred to the army.[65]

Naval Forces

Little has been written on the role and performance of the Russian navy in the war with Georgia. As mentioned in the introduction to this monograph, the Russian naval force was built around the cruiser, *Moskva*, and the destroyer, *Smetlivy*, and included two battalions of naval infantry, which landed on the coast of Abkhazia and from there moved into Georgia proper. Three landing ships appear to have been used in the amphibious operation: the *Caesar Kunikov*, *Jamal*, and *Saratov*.[66] Although the landing was successful, this tells us little about Russian amphibious capability, since it was unopposed. Subsequent Russian statements in justification of Russia's planned purchase of *Mistral*-class amphibious landing ships from France have made reference to the fact that the Russian landing in Abkhazia could have been completed much more quickly and effectively with *Mistral*-class ships.

There is little that can be learned in the way of Russian surface-warfare capabilities from the war. Although Russia claimed that its naval vessels *Mirazh* and *Suzdalets* sank a Georgian patrol boat that threatened the Black Sea Fleet as it approached the coast of Abkhazia, Georgia does not acknowledge the loss of a patrol boat and makes no mention of any naval action against the Black Sea Fleet in its official timeline of the war.[67] Russian forces did eventually destroy several Georgian navy ships at anchor in Poti where they were based, after the two sides declared a ceasefire. The Georgian coast guard, which had received significant U.S. training and equipment and was thus in many ways more capable than the navy, relocated from Poti south to the port of Batumi in order to preserve its vessels.

Special Forces and Irregular Forces

There has been little analysis of the role of Russian special forces in the war. Georgian reports mention several instances in which Russian helicopters inserted troops in black uniforms behind Georgian lines, where they may have engaged in subversion and espionage.[68] There are a number of reports in the Russian media that Russian special forces (GRU) units operated in Georgian territory. The veracity of these reports is unknown. What is known is that North Caucasus volunteer forces—especially the Chechen "East" and "West" Battalions—as well as South Ossetian and Abkhazian militia forces, played significant roles in the war. All of the irregular forces, both those from Russia and those from the separatist provinces, were deployed prior to the outbreak of the war and likely conducted reconnaissance and advance-guard operations for their Russian allies.

In South Ossetia, Georgian officers contend that militia forces deployed in Tskhinvali continually harassed Georgian forces as they moved through the town.[69] Foreign analysts agree that these forces appear to have engaged in standard partisan operations—using small hit-and-run engagements where their chances of survival were higher and using civilian clothing to blend in with the local population.[70] South Ossetian militia forces and the Chechen battalions also conducted some of the most egregious ethnic cleansing in the wake of the war, burning ethnic Georgian villages in South Ossetia and ejecting their inhabitants. The EU, the United Nations (UN), and several human rights organizations documented this ethnic cleansing and criticized the Russian military for its inability or unwillingness to control forces it had trained and which were fighting alongside it.

Abkhazian military forces were significantly better organized and equipped than were those from South Ossetia. The Abkhazian ground forces were organized into three motorized rifle brigades and a separate artillery regiment, and were equipped with Russian-made tanks, armored personnel carriers, howitzers, and rocket launchers of various types. The total personnel strength of the Abkhazian armed forces—including the small air and naval forces—was around 10,000. Although Georgian forces did not move into Abkhazia as they did in South Ossetia, there was a small Georgian force in the Kodori Gorge (Upper Abkhazia). Abkhaz military with Russian artillery and air support were able to dislodge this force and seize the gorge.

Logistical Support and Strategic Mobility

While the strategic mobility system generally performed as advertised, as is evidenced by the landings of troops in Abkhazia by the Black Sea Fleet and the 100-plus transport sorties that were flown to ferry troops to the theater of operations in South Ossetia, Russian forces proved less proficient in operational and tactical logistics. Despite the short duration of the war and the relatively small area over which it was fought, there are indications that the Russian ground logistics system was severely taxed.

The former Georgian Deputy Defense Minister remarked that the Georgian side was aware of serious Russian problems keeping up with the demand for food, fuel, and ammunition. Some Georgian officials believe that one of the reasons the Russian army halted its advance at the town of Igoeti, some 30 kilometers from the capital of Tbilisi, was its logistical incapability of advancing further.[71] First-hand Russian accounts support this picture of a logistics system unable to cope with the demands placed on it. A Russian tank commander explained the destruction of two of his tanks in the village of Zemo-Nikozi thus: "We simply ran out of ammunition, and they surrounded us with grenade launchers."[72]

Cyber Warfare and Information Operations

The area of cyber warfare and information operations is one of the most illuminating areas of study in this conflict. The war against Georgia marks the first time in its history that Russia has used cyber war and information operations in support of its conventional operations. The Russian cyber campaign attacked a total of 38 Georgian and Western websites upon the outbreak of the war, including those of the Georgian President, the Ministry of Foreign Affairs, the National Bank, the Parliament, the Supreme Court, and the U.S. and United Kingdom (UK) embassies in Georgia.

These attacks appear to have been centrally directed and coordinated, judging from the fact that they started and ended within 30 minutes of one another—beginning at about 5:15 p.m. on August 8 and ending at about 12:45 p.m. on August 11, at the time when Russia announced its ceasefire.[73]

Despite this fact, it is unlikely that the attacks were conducted directly by the Russian government. Although Russia has been a source of many of the most sophisticated cyber attacks in recent years, most of these are thought to originate from a shadowy group called the Russian Business Network (RBN), which has not been definitively shown to have links to the Russian government. Indeed, the fact that the RBN is not a registered company and that its internet domains are registered to anonymous addresses makes pinning down the origins and ownership of the RBN a challenge for the intelligence community. In any case, the RBN is notorious for cybercrimes such as identity theft, phishing, spam, and malware distribution, but it has also specialized, among other bad deeds, in the type of distributed denial of service (DDOS) attacks that were aimed at Georgian websites during the war.[74] In an earlier spat between Russia and Estonia over the removal of a Soviet war memorial from the Estonian capital, the Estonian government was subjected to a similar series of attacks also thought to have been conducted by the RBN. The most likely scenario in both cases is that RBN conducted the attacks on behalf of the Russian government, providing the government with plausible deniability.

Interestingly, the cyber attacks on Georgia were less effective than they might have been against a more wired government. Although the Georgian internet infrastructure proved relatively simple for Russian cyber warriors to overwhelm, the Georgian government proved adept at getting itself back up online. The Georgian President's website was reestablished as a page on the website of the President of Poland, which Russia proved unable or unwilling to attack; other Georgian government websites quickly reestablished themselves as blogs behind the protection of *google*, and again Russia was unwilling or unable to bring them down. The result was an explosion in the size and importance of the Georgian blogosphere, which has continued to be a thorn in Russia's side since the end of the war.[75] A final reason that Russian cyber attacks were limited in their effectiveness is that in August 2008 Georgia had only recently set up official email accounts for its government and military. At the start of the war, many, if not most, Georgian officials still used their personal accounts (gmail, yahoo, etc.) for official communication, meaning that attacks on Georgian government email servers had little effect on their ability to communicate.

Concurrent with the cyber war against Georgia was a Russian attempt to seize the initiative in the information war by ensuring that its narrative dominated the discussion of the causes and results of the conflict. The Russian narrative consistently emphasized three major themes: first, Georgia in general and President Saakashvili in particular were the aggressors; second, Russia was forced to intervene in defense of its citizens and to prevent a humanitarian catastrophe; and finally, the United States and the West had no basis on which to criticize Russia because of Western actions in Kosovo and elsewhere.[76] Vendel and Westerlund echo these themes, writing that a key part of the Russian strategy was to appear to be the victim and not the initiator of the war, which is consistent with Soviet/ Russian narratives in Afghanistan and Chechnya.[77]

Key elements of this narrative took hold, especially the idea that Russian actions were defensive in nature and that Georgia was the aggressor. Even after extensive evidence came to light from multiple sources that Russian forces had entered South Ossetia prior to the outbreak of war, the idea that Georgia moved first and Russia responded persisted. Perhaps the clearest evidence of this mindset appears in the official EU report on the conflict. While acknowledging that there is ample evidence that Russian forces entered South Ossetia prior to the Georgian intervention, the report surprisingly argues that there was not enough information about the number and activities of Russian forces to conclude definitively that an invasion was underway. This should lead to a conclusion that intelligence available to the EU was of a poor quality. However, the EU report concludes that Georgia's deployment into South Ossetia was illegal under international law.

In addition to having a narrative prepared and effectively propagating it in the early days of the war, Russia seems to have been significantly savvier in dealing with the media than it had been in previous conflicts, especially those in Chechnya. Russian General Staff briefers appeared to have studied U.S. briefings from the wars in Iraq and Afghanistan and attempted to model their performances on these. The Russian government also demonstrated an increased willingness to work with the Russian media, as evidenced by the fact that it flew some 50 reporters to Tskhinvali several days prior to the outbreak of the war—another indication that the Russian attack was imminent.[78] It also effectively used Russian television to portray Georgia as a Western surrogate by showing U.S. equipment from the recently concluded exercise Immediate Response '08 as "proof" that American forces had assisted the Georgians in planning and executing their intervention in South Ossetia.[79] Russian interactions with Western media were less frequent, and Russian officials repeatedly complained that Georgian officials—especially President Saakashvili— were given too much air time on Western networks.

So the preplanned and relentlessly propagated Russian narrative of Georgian aggression and Russian response was relatively successful in dominating early discourse on the war. But there were elements of the Russian narrative that were heavy-handed and poorly considered. The most obvious of these is the claim of Georgian genocide against South Ossetia, which Russian and South Ossetian sources claimed had resulted in 1,400-2,000 civilian casualties. Although this figure was often repeated by Western media in the early days of the war, it was later rejected by multiple independent investigations, which put the number of South Ossetian civilian casualties in the 100-133 range and acknowledged that a number of these were probably South Ossetian fighters in civilian clothes.[80]

There was a backlash from the extreme nature of some Russian claims about the war and the heavy-handed way in which they were delivered. Ordinary Russians who wanted a break from the distorted and one-sided accounts of the situation in Georgia provided by Russian television began to turn to the inter-net, where a lively, two-sided and uncensored debate ensued.[81] Even experts at Moscow State University found themselves unable to get reliable information on the war from Russian sources and began turning to Radio Free Europe/Radio Liberty for updates.[82] In summary, then, although the Russian narrative dominated the discourse in the early days of the war and although the Russian government and military proved more adept at handling the media than in previous conflicts, the Russian information operations strategy was limited in its effectiveness due to a lack of subtlety and believability in key parts of its message.

RUSSIAN LESSONS LEARNED IN THE WAR WITH GEORGIA

Despite the fact that the war with Georgia resulted in a victory for Russia, the performance of the Russian military in the war has been the subject of significant discussion and criticism in the almost 2 years since the war ended. President Dmitri Medvedev himself named five areas of reform that must be emphasized going forward: bringing all combat formations to permanent-readiness status (i.e., elimination of cadre units); raising the effectiveness of command and control systems; improving the system of officer training; upgrading equipment with a focus on PGMs; and improving pay, housing, and social amenities for *kontraktniky* and officers.[83] Approaching the problem from a different level, Lieutenant General Vladimir Shamanov, former Chief of the Main Combat Training and Service Directorate, identified the key problems exposed by the war as poor interoperability between the air force and ground forces, poor communications capabilities, and the low resolution of Russian reconnaissance systems, especially UAVs.[84]

As Mikhail Barabanov, editor and co-author of *Tanks of August*, noted,

> Though from the position of unsophisticated extraneous observers one saw a quick, massive and decisive action of the Russian army and successful crushing of the Georgian armed forces, in reality, as became completely clear, the experience of the utilization of the Russian armed forces in conflict was considered sufficiently contradictory by the political-military leadership of the RF, which led in the end to a new stage of radical military reform, the one which has as its goal bringing the armed forces of the country to a "new look," oriented, first of all, towards participation in local conflicts in the territory of the former USSR.[85]

An adviser to the Minister of Defense of Russia told Dr. Cohen that the war confirmed that Russia needs to spend most of its efforts and procurement funds on building a smaller, more maneuverable, and rapidly deployable army to defend its borders, not fight a world war. "This is where the money goes, despite losing over 50 percent of the budget to graft."[86] Finally, Russian military analysts have concluded that although the war validated the concept of joint operations, it also demonstrated that the Russian armed forces have a long way to go before they are capable of operating in a truly joint manner. Readiness was a major issue as well—a survey of the Russian military completed after the war showed that only 17 percent of army units and 5 out of 150 air force regiments were combat-ready.[87] Thus, the requirements for reform dictated by Russian performance in the war with Georgia are ample and fundamental, and seem to be acknowledged by both the political and military leadership of the country.

Equipment

All services in the Russian armed forces experienced considerable problems with equipment during the war. For the ground forces, the reliability of their armored vehicles seemed to be the most troubling issue related to equipment. But survivability was also an issue, in part due to lack of reactive armor, but also due simply to the low quality of Russian-made armored vehicles, which proved much more vulnerable than their Western counterparts to aircraft, artillery, other armored vehicles, and shoulder-fired anti-armor weapons. Finally, the lack of night vision capability proved another significant problem.

For the air force, the lack of an effective and reliable anti-radar missile proved fatal for Russia's ability to conduct effective SEAD. A lack of reliable, all-weather PGMs was also a significant equipment-related weakness, as was the lack of equipment designed to allow Russian aircraft to operate at night. Finally, the Russian ability to conduct close air support was eroded by the lack of radios interoperable with those in the Russian ground forces.

Although the Russian navy was not tested in the war with Georgia, Russian analysts and military leaders have remarked that the landing on the coast of Abkhazia, which proved difficult even though unopposed, highlighted the need for improvements in the area of amphibious landing platforms. The limitations in this capability exposed by the war were certainly part of the reason for Russia's recent decision to buy *Mistral*-class ships from France. The *Mistral*, a multi-role ship capable of transporting and deploying 16 helicopters, 70 armored vehicles, and up to 450 personnel, represents a significant improvement over current Russian helicopter carriers and landing craft. However, internal bickering over budgets and rampant corruption may still derail the shift to acquisition of foreign surface combatants, which made up the bulk of the czarist navy prior to World War I.

One of the areas in which Russian deficiencies were most starkly demonstrated was that of command, control, communications, computers, intelligence, surveillance and reconnaissance (C4ISR), which has been bluntly described as unsatisfactory by military analysts.[88] The aforementioned lack of interoperability between the radio systems of different services and the vulnerability of Russian radios to electronic warfare led Russian commanders to rely on mobile phones for a considerable portion of their command and control requirements during the war. Although this in itself is bad enough, the fact that these calls went over Georgian mobile phone networks, which are the primary networks serving South Ossetia,[89] makes the problem even more significant from a communications security standpoint.

The criticality of satellite imagery, navigation, and guidance was also amply demonstrated during the war. The fact that GLONASS was not fielded and that GPS data were disrupted—presumably at the request of the United States—led to massive problems in selecting targets for the air campaign and in delivering precision strikes on Georgian targets. It may also have adversely affected the Russian SEAD effort; Roger McDermott attributes the Russian failure to make use of anti-radar missiles to the lack of GLONASS or GPS guidance.[90] The lack of a satellite navigation capability also presumably led to operational security breaches as units used radios or—more likely—mobile phones to report their positions to their higher headquarters, rather than higher headquarters simply following the positions of all of its units on a digital map. These shortcomings help explain why in September 2008 Russian Prime Minister Putin announced an increase in funding for GLONASS by 67 billion rubles (approximately $2.4 billion).[91]

Doctrine, Training, and Personnel

As President Medvedev's five areas of emphasis noted above make clear, the experience of the war showed that doctrine, training, and personnel make up a considerable portion of the systems in need of reform. In this realm, special focus has been put on the following areas: transition to a contract (professional) force; reorganization of the ground forces from the old military district and division-based system to a brigade-based system; elimination of cadre units; improvements in officer training; and improvements in social and living conditions, especially for junior service members. The catalysts for all of these changes can be found in the experience of the war with Georgia.

Although the transition to a contract force has encountered some resistance from senior Russian military officers, the fact that Russia was forced to send conscripts into combat in violation of official policy and the fact that many of these conscripts performed poorly, led the Russian leadership to see expanding the percentage of contract soldiers in the armed forces as a necessity. Moreover, the Russian military district and division-based structure proved inflexible in responding to the requirements of a short, mid-intensity war along Russia's border. The 76th Air Assault Division, for example, needed to be split into two task-organized units, with one sent to South Ossetia and the other to Abkhazia. The Russian reform effort—much like that of its U.S. predecessor—envisions permanent task-organized brigade-sized units with all enablers assigned, providing significantly greater flexibility.

The drive to eliminate cadre units, the next area of emphasis, stems directly from the fact that during the war the leadership of these units proved generally unsatisfactory, due to lack of experience in commanding actual troops and the fact that the requirements to staff cadre units led to a depletion of personnel from first-line units. The fourth area of emphasis—the poor tactical performance of many Russian units—amply demonstrated the need to improve the system of officer training. And finally, improving social and living standards has long been an imperative within the Russian military, but little has been done about it. However, once Russian soldiers saw the living conditions of Georgian soldiers in bases like Senaki and Gori, they became livid at their own squalid conditions—as a much-circulated mobile phone video of the expletive-laden tirade of several Russian soldiers inside the Georgian barracks at Senaki makes clear.

Cyber Warfare and Information Warfare

Since the war with Georgia marked the first use of cyber warfare and information operations in conjunction with a conventional military operation, this area proved fertile ground for Russian lessons learned. In the area of cyber warfare, Russian denial-of-services attacks on Georgian websites were effective early in preventing the Georgian government from getting its message out, and the fact that these attacks were likely orchestrated by the Russian Business Network gave the Russian government a veneer of deniability. However, the pressure that these attacks put on the Georgian government resulted in two adverse consequences apparently unforeseen by Russian planners—first, the rise of the Georgian blogosphere, which proved difficult if not impossible to attack due to its diffuse nature and lack of a central node of control; and second, the increased use of television—especially Western television channels—by the Georgian government to get its message out. On television, Georgia's young, Western-educated political leadership generally made a better impression on Western audiences than did their Russian counterparts, even though Russian spokesmen and diplomats have made considerable strides in this area.

The information war contained three main lessons for Russian political and military leaders. First is the need to verify accusations made against the enemy or to moderate them if verification is impossible. An example of this is Russian claims of a Georgian-perpetrated "genocide" in Tskhinvali. The original accusations came from South Ossetian officials, but their Russian counterparts echoed them immediately, thereby lending them more credence than they would otherwise have had. When these claims were later definitely disproven—and in fact it was proven by multiple independent investigations that Georgian villages in South Ossetia suffered significantly greater damage and that their residents were systematically driven out—Russian claims of genocide by Georgia began to look hypocritical, to say the least.

The next lesson learned in the information war is that embedded reporters are a double-edged sword. While they can be effective at putting a human face on the Russian military effort and in telling the Russian side of the story, they can also undermine the information strategy. First, the fact that the Russian government flew some 50 embedded reporters to Tskhinvali days before the outbreak of the war, where they were seen by a photographer for Radio Free Europe/Radio Liberty when he arrived on August 5 for a previously scheduled photo shoot,[92] casts doubt upon the Russian narrative that Russian peacekeepers and South Ossetian civilians were the innocent and unsuspecting victims of Georgian aggression on August 8. Embedded reporters can also serve as conduits for the release of information on the locations and activities of the units they are embedded with. Aside from being an obvious security risk (think of Geraldo Rivera drawing with his stick in the sand of the Iraqi desert), it can be especially damaging if this information contradicts the official narrative of events, as was the case with the multiple reports in the Russian-language press of Russian units entering South Ossetia prior to the outbreak of the war.

The final lesson learned in the information war is the ubiquity of cameras of all types on the battlefield. Soldiers, journalists, and civilians carrying mobile phones—almost all of which now have relatively capable video camera apps—are a constant and omnipresent potential source of unfiltered content straight from the battlefield to the internet. Three vignettes serve to illustrate the effects of this phenomenon. The first is the mobile phone video with the audible sound of Russian soldiers going through the Georgian barracks in Senaki, and their obvious surprise and anger in finding that the army they have just beaten lives better than they do in every conceivable category. The second is the mobile phone video of Georgian soldiers in their armored vehicles moving through Tskhinvali on the morning of August 8. The fact that the town was deserted, but intact—with smoke visible from only one building—cast early doubt on the Russian claims that Georgia had subjected it to massive and indiscriminate artillery bombardment the night before.

Finally, there is the video taken by a journalist of Russian 58th Army Commander Khruliev pounding the ground with his fist and lamenting the loss of virtually his entire command group after it rolled into an ambush by Georgian forces. Western military forces have extensive experience with the issues of message management, embedded reporters, and ubiquitous cameras on the battlefield, and still struggle with them; it is therefore unlikely that Russia, with much less experience, will remain immune from the effects of embedded reporting in future conflicts.

MILITARY MODERNIZATION 2 YEARS LATER

Despite the inevitable resistance to radical change from some quarters of the Russian military and the effects of bureaucratic inertia on Russian reform plans, a fair amount has been accomplished in the almost 2 years since the end of the war between Russia and Georgia. Reform efforts began with personnel and force structure changes and are only now beginning to move in the direction of modernizing equipment and reforming procurement procedures. Russian observers have noted that the reforms of the Russian forces in the North Caucasus Military district caused the following outcomes:

- Decrease in number of tank and mechanized infantry battalions;
- Disorganization of the old cadre system;
- Decrease in number of attack aircraft near Georgian borders with some expansion of possibilities for immediate troop [aerial] support, due to the creation of front and army aviation air bases in Abkhazia and South Ossetia and beginning of rearmament of army aviation with new helicopters; and,
- Decrease in opportunities to beef up the military group in the Caucasus quickly with the help of other military districts and air assault troops, due to a decrease in the number of military cargo planes.

At the same time, the process of rearmament of North Caucasus units with new and more modern systems is supposed to compensate for the decrease in their numbers. Moreover, the strengthening of war-fighting capabilities of the Russian troops based in Armenia will allow them to be used for an attack on Tbilisi-Marneuli from the south, and/or [for an attack] against Javakheti and further against Adjara.[93]

Despite substantial budget increases, the impact of corruption on the reform process makes its successful completion an unsure and expensive prospect.

Personnel and Force Structure

Initial Russian military reform efforts focused on personnel and force structure changes. Given the cuts in the officer corps envisioned, it is no surprise that these efforts met with resistance from elements of the Russian military leadership. Initial resistance emanated primarily from retired generals and officers, the General Staff ,and military educational institutions, the number of which was slated to be cut from 65 to 10.[94] Additionally, reform plans called for the discharge of some 200,000 officers and 120,000 warrant officers, and a reduction in the overall number of Army units from 1,890 to 172.[95] Despite resentment from within the ranks of the military and delays due to the need to provide housing for discharged service members, these reforms have largely been completed. Current areas of emphasis are the introduction of a new salary scale and the development of a professional noncommissioned officer corps.

The new Russian military is being reduced in strength from 1.3 million men to 1.0 million and will use the brigade as its principal combat formation, having eliminated the regimental and divisional levels of command. This new military structure is thought to be more useful in the regional and local types of conflicts Russia envisions itself fighting over the short and mid term. Minister of Defense Anatoly Serdiukov remarked in December 2008 that the objective of the reforms is to allow Russia to prosecute three of these types of conflicts simultaneously.[96] Russian troops will also form the core of the 5,000-man rapid reaction force of the Collective Security Treaty Organization (CSTO, the security arm of the CIS), which Russia hopes to turn into a rival to NATO by establishing it as the preeminent security pact in the post-Soviet space.

Procurement and Budgeting

Having completed the bulk of the personnel and force structure reforms, Russia is now shifting focus to equipment modernization. As noted earlier, among the unpleasant surprises for Russian troops and leaders in the war with Georgia was the fact that Georgian equipment was often better than that of the Russians themselves. The recent promotion of Colonel-General (Retired) Vladimir Popovkin to the post of First Deputy Defense Minister portends a shift in focus from equipping the force to reorganizing it, and also a greater Russian willingness to purchase military equipment from foreign firms. Popovkin had been Chief of the Armaments Directorate of the Russian Ministry of Defense; his promotion signals not so much a shift in his responsibilities as an elevation of the procurement portfolio within the Ministry of Defense. Indeed, in announcing his promotion to First Deputy Minister, President Medvedev instructed him to "coordinate rearmament and procurement, and put into practice the new state armament program that is being finalized at present."[97] Medvedev also directed him to crack down on defense contractors that "make mischief" by inflating prices,[98] an acknowledgment that even with rising defense budgets, Russia must get more bang for its procurement buck if it hopes to modernize and avoid falling farther behind the West in the quality of its armaments.

Earlier, Medvedev had announced the new weapons systems and platforms that will enter service with the Russian armed forces in 2009-10; these include five Iskander-M ballistic missile systems with 300 ballistic missiles, 300 tanks and armored vehicles, 30 helicopters, 28 combat aircraft, 3 nuclear submarines, one corvette, and 11 satellites. While the numbers might be impressive, they fail to convey the fact that this new equipment will still be based on late-Soviet designs that have been around for at least the last 10- 15 years.[99] For the Russian military to truly transform into a 21st century force, it must procure 21st century equipment (and train soldiers to use it), but—except in rare cases—the Russian defense industry is incapable of producing equipment of this caliber.

The second reason for the importance of Popovkin's promotion is that it signals that the recent Russian willingness to purchase key capabilities from foreign firms has support at the highest levels of the Russian government. Popovkin was among the first of senior Russian officials to advocate purchasing military equipment abroad. In January 2008—even before the war with Georgia—Popovkin became the first Russian military official to disclose publicly that Russia was using foreign electronic components in its military satellites, and in July of that year, he announced that the French firm Thales had been awarded a contract to provide Russian T90S tanks with night vision infrared television cameras.[100] The war with Georgia convinced much of Russia's leadership that Popovkin's instincts were correct—that there were certain capabilities that were so important to the creation of a technologically advanced military force that they must be purchased from the best available source, regardless of country of origin.

Many Russian military and political leaders agreed with Popovkin's assessment that the Russian defense industry would not be spurred to develop better systems unless it were subjected to competition from foreign firms. In September 2009, Popovkin announced to representatives of Russian defense firms that the Ministry of Defense would purchase equipment abroad if they could not provide it. Later that month the Ministry signed a contract with an Israeli firm for the purchase of UAVs.[101] Given the abysmal performance of the Russian-made Pchela UAV in the war with Georgia—Russian commanders said the images it sent were so poor, they were useless and it "flew so low you could hit it with a slingshot and [it] roared like a BTR"[102]—it is unsurprising that Russia chose to seek a foreign vendor for this key platform. In September 2010, Israeli Defense Minister Ehud Barak and his Russian counterpart, Anatoly Serdyukov, signed the first military cooperation agreement between Russia and Israel. Under the agreement, Israel will provide Russia the UAV and other technology.[103] This decision represents a shift from the long-standing Soviet and Russian practice to source virtually all military equipment from domestic producers.

All indications are that purchases of equipment from foreign sources will accelerate. In addition to the UAV purchase from Israel, which could total $300- 400 million and which Russia hopes will lead to an agreement to produce UAVs under license on Russian soil,[104] there is the previously mentioned tender to supply an amphibious landing/helicopter carrier ship, which *Mistral*-class ships from France are likely to win. Russia is also attempting to turn this deal into a licensed-production agreement, allowing it to produce some or all parts of the ships domestically after an initial purchase of one or two French-made *Mistrals*.[105] Finally, Popovkin recently announced that Russia is negotiating to buy German armor for Russian combat vehicles and technical support to produce it domestically.[106]

A more professional, more mobile, and better equipped force means a more expensive force. Accordingly, the Russian military budget has climbed precipitously in recent years, rising by 27 percent to $50 billion from 2008 to 2009 alone, marking a 10-fold increase in defense spending since 2000.[107] But even with these gaudy rates of increase, Russia is still attempting to maintain a force only 20 percent smaller than that of the U.S. military on a budget 1/15th the size of the U.S. defense budget.[108] Even with the shift toward equipping the force with modern systems, procurement accounts for only 30 percent of the Russian defense budget, compared to 54 percent in the United States.[109]

To make matters worse, the impact of corruption on the Russian defense budget is enormous—retired General Alexander Kanshin says up to 30 percent of the budget is stolen or misused,[110] and other Russian military officials have in confidence asserted that the figure might be even higher.[111] Given these conditions—a rising but still small budget for the size of the force, a smaller percentage of that budget devoted to procurement than in the United States, and the corrosive impact of corruption—it is highly uncertain whether Russia's drive for modernization of its military equipment will be successful, lessons of the Georgian war notwithstanding.

CHANGES IN RUSSIAN MILITARY DOCTRINE

The recently released 2010 Russian military doctrine represents an attempt to integrate lessons from the war with Georgia—both political and military— and use them where they advance Russia's conception of itself as a power once again on the rise. However, where the lessons of the Georgia war come into conflict with entrenched organizational interests within the Russian military, Russia's doctrine writers proved less willing to integrate these lessons into the document. In the end, given Russia's limited resources and expanding ambitions, there are four key balances that the new doctrine must strike: between preparing for internal and regional conflicts and preparing for conflicts with other great powers; between training for counterinsurgency and training for conventional military operations; between a legacy 20th century force and a 21st century force; and between a professional and a conscript force.

Internal and Regional Versus Major Conflicts

The balance between preparing for internal and regional conflicts versus preparing for larger conflicts is an area in which Russia's Great Power ambitions and its nostalgia for its Cold War sense of superpower status clash with its current threats and geopolitical situation. An increasingly violent North Caucasus, instability in Central Asia, and the rise of China all point to a need for Russia to configure itself to fight small- to mid-sized wars along its borders. However, the new doctrine cannot quite rid itself of the idea that the primary danger to Russia comes from NATO. While NATO has been downgraded from a "threat" to a "military danger," which the doctrine defines as a situation that can under certain circumstances develop into a threat, NATO's capacity to act globally and its enlargement still warrant special mention.[112] Other dangers listed are the deployment of foreign forces on territory adjacent to Russia and its allies, the development of missile defense systems on proximate foreign soil, and the creation of strategic nonnuclear weapons[113]—all clear references to U.S. or Western activities or programs. China merits no mention in the doctrine.[114]

The new doctrine also continues to promote a long-standing Russian goal—the (re-) establishment of spheres of influence in the former Soviet area. Indeed, Medvedev himself foreshadowed this when on August 31, 2008, he gave a television address asserting that Russia has a "zone of privileged interests" along its periphery where it would operate in defense of its interests without submitting its actions to international institutions for discussion or approval. The new doctrine echoes this theme by advocating a "division of zones of responsibility between NATO and the CSTO and expanding the Russian President's authority to deploy forces abroad without prior consultation with parliament.[115]

Interestingly, when presented with what would seem to have been a golden opportunity to assert these newly minted privileges, after the interim Kyrgyz government requested Russia to deploy forces to quell ethnic violence in the Fergana Valley in June 2010, Russia not only declined to do so unilaterally but failed to press the CSTO to do so. This may indicate that Russian military interventions in the Near Abroad are as much directed at the West as they are at the country in which the intervention takes place. In Kyrgyzstan, despite the presence of a U.S. air base, the United States made it clear from the outset that it had no plans to deploy peacekeeping or stability forces, and Kyrgyzstan's geographic, economic, and security situations keep it dependent upon Russia to a considerable extent. Russia may therefore have concluded it had nothing to gain by deploying forces to Kyrgyzstan and nothing to lose by failing to do so.

Contrasted with this recent restraint in its self-proclaimed "zone of privileged interests" is Russia's behavior further afield. Russia has been busy establishing new anchorages and naval bases far from the waters of the Russian Federation. It has recently deployed naval forces to Tartus/Latakiye (Syria), Venezuela, and Cuba and has discussed establishing a permanent presence in the Indian Ocean and Red Sea, where it currently participates in the anti-piracy operation. Russian aircraft have also expanded air patrols on both the Atlantic and Pacific, at times harassing foreign ships and aircraft or probing foreign airspace.[116]

Thus, although the new Russian military doctrine explicitly lists NATO enlargement, not the West as a whole, as a danger, both the doctrine and Russian behavior seem to confirm that, in striking a balance between preparing to fight internal and small regional wars and preparing to confront the West, Russia's military imperatives and its political desires are at odds. While Russian military and political leaders certainly understand that the violent North Caucasus, an unstable Central Asia, and a rising China argue for the development of forces capable of fighting local and regional wars (and these forces are in fact being developed), Russia's old Cold Warriors cannot quite rid themselves of the notion that the West is a dangerous potential enemy that bears watching and that its overtures to Russia's neighbors constitute infringements on Russia's alleged special privileges in these countries.

Counterinsurgency Versus Conventional Military Operations

While the first balance the new doctrine attempts to strike is between the types of threats Russia faces, the second one is between the types of forces it requires to meet those threats. If Russia's military situation and its geopolitical ambitions are in tension in the first case, in this case its military requirements and its procurement system appear to sometimes be working at cross purposes. Given that the primary near- and mid-term threats to Russian security come from internal insurgency in the North Caucasus and regional instability in the former Soviet Union, one would expect the new doctrine to emphasize the development of highly capable counterinsurgency forces and mobile forces capable of conducting limited but fast-paced joint and highly lethal operations along Russia's periphery. Indeed, a senior Russian military official remarked recently that what Russia is attempting to develop is a "small, professional army for Russia's periphery."[117] The new doctrine echoes this by providing for the use of Russian forces abroad to "protect the interests of the Russian Federation and its citizens."[118]

But a review of Russia's recent procurement priorities does not necessarily support this objective. Recall that prominent among Russia's deliveries in 2009-10 were ballistic missiles, tanks, nuclear submarines, and surface ships. In addition, the new doctrine and recent Russian military budgets continue to devote considerable resources to Russia's strategic nuclear forces. All of these legacy systems compete for scarce resources with the forces and capabilities Russia needs for the army it claims to be building. There is an argument to be made that the procurement timeline is so long that these items were already in the pipeline long before Russia's new doctrine was published. While this may be the case, the same cannot be said of Russia's foreign procurements. Some of these—UAVs, upgraded armor, and night vision devices—are clearly designed to assist in developing smaller, more mobile, and more lethal forces for counterinsurgency and regional conflicts, but others—the *Mistral*-class ships, by far the most expensive of the foreign purchases—seem designed to give Russia a conventional power projection capability of dubious use in fighting insurgents and local wars along its periphery.

20th Century Versus 21st Century Warfare

Military analysts like Margarete Klein and Roger McDermott have correctly noted that the Russia-Georgia War was the last "20th century" war Russia is likely to fight. Russian leaders seemed to understand this, and they therefore embarked on the effort currently underway to shed cumbersome 20th-century military formations like the military district and the division, to reform military staffs and the educational system with the goal of streamlining decisionmaking and encouraging leaders to take initiative, and to procure modern, 21st-century military equipment. Despite this, the new doctrine completely fails to mention these reform processes. As Keir Giles says, "It is impossible to overstate the magnitude of the upheaval, and of the shift in operational assumptions, that have shaken the Russian military over the last 13 months; nevertheless the new doctrine reflects the *status quo ante*."[119]

In some areas the new doctrine does backhandedly acknowledge that there have been changes, but it neither clarifies nor endorses them. For instance, while the new doctrine deletes the portion of the 2000 doctrine that clarified the role of the Ministry of Defense, the General Staff, and the military districts, it does not replace it.[120] In other words, the new document is simply mute on the issue of who does what at the highest levels of the Russian military. It is possible that the long-bureaucratized process of doctrine writing failed to keep up with the pace of reform, and that the pressure to release the new military doctrine resulted in a decision to release it "as is" rather than attempt to secure approval from all stakeholders for comprehensive changes at the 11th hour.

It is also possible that the failure to detail the comprehensive reform processes underway are an attempt to undermine them. In this view, the authors of the new doctrine, opponents of the reforms like many high-ranking officers in the Russian military, decided that withholding any mention of the reforms in a published military doctrine might make them simpler to reverse when the time is right. In any case, it is curious that the most comprehensive military reforms undertaken in the Russian military in generations, reforms designed to turn the

Russian armed forces into a 21st-century fighting force, drew no mention whatsoever in the first 21st-century Russian military doctrine.

Professional Versus Conscript Force

This area is another one in which the objectives of Russian political leaders have met resistance from its military bureaucracy. As mentioned previously, in the war with Georgia the Russian military was forced to violate its own policy by deploying conscripts to a military operation on foreign soil. In addition, even Russian *kontraktniky* often proved poorly trained and incapable of the type of fast-paced, independent operations required in this war, forcing the better trained airborne and special forces units to do much of the fighting.[121] Paul Rich maintains that even as raw material the *kontraktniky* proved less than optimal—many of them turned out to be in poor health and/or barely educated, since they came primarily from rural and economically disadvantaged backgrounds.[122]

Perhaps reflecting these shortcomings, the new doctrine is less ambitious in its vision for the replacement of conscripts with *kontraktniky*. Whereas the previous objective had been a fully professionalized Russian military, the new doctrine simply states that formations and military units should "in the majority" be manned by professional soldiers.[123] Some Western military analysts have opined that the current consensus within the Russian military is that the experiment with professionalization of the armed forces has failed and that Russia will return to a largely conscript force.[124] Whatever the source of the newfound unease among some in the Russian military with transition to a fully professional force, what is clear is that Russia's stated intention to transform its military to enable it to meet 21st-century challenges is at odds with the maintenance of conscription. By most accounts, distortions and corruption in Russia's conscription system mean that the quality of conscripts entering the Russian armed forces will remain generally worse than the quality of Russian *kontraktniki*.

In summary, then, the new Russian military doctrine attempts to square the lessons of the Georgia war with traditional Russian geopolitical objectives and entrenched organizational interests within the Russian military. Given the impossibility of doing so completely, the document that emerges from the effort is often pragmatic, although at times far-fetched and even self-contradictory. It is worthwhile for U.S. policymakers to study the reasons for, and conduct of, the war, as well as the resulting changes in the military doctrine, procurement, and geopolitical behavior connected to the Russo-Georgian hostilities.

The long-term outcomes of the current Russia-Georgia war will be felt far and wide, from Afghanistan to Iran and from the Caspian to the Mediterranean. The war was an earthquake, indicating that the geopolitical tectonic plates are shifting, and nations in Eurasia, as well as U.S. policymakers, need to take notice.

GEOPOLITICAL LESSONS FROM THE WAR

Lessons from the Russia-Georgia war abound, and apply both to grand strategy, military operations, cyber warfare, and strategic information operations. The most important of these are:

- Russian continental power is on the rise. In 2008 Russia was willing, and may be willing again in the future, to change the borders of Europe by force, making the 1975 Helsinki Accords obsolete. Moscow justifies this policy by citing Kosovo and other Yugoslav examples. The war is intricately linked with Russia's demands to revise European security architecture, do away with NATO, and weaken the U.S. security presence in, and ties with, Europe. The 20-year-long post-Cold War era of joint attempts between NATO and Russia to build a joint European security architecture has come to an end.[125]

- The war undermined the close relationships the United States had developed with post-Soviet states since the collapse of the Soviet Union. Small states treat nuclear- and conventionally-armed great powers with respect. In addition, the historic memory of the past imperial domination plays a role in the attitudes of peripheral elites towards the former metropolis' geopolitical agendas: the former imperial master is often nine feet tall. Provoking a militarily strong great power, such as Russia, China, or Iran, is clearly dangerous. Saakashvili's is an example that many leaders in the post-Soviet space are understandably reluctant to follow, remembering it in their dealings with Moscow.

- Expressions of U.S. support are an insufficient deterrent short of NATO membership or a separate mutual defense pact. U.S. expressions of support provided to Georgia (clearly, short of an explicit mutual defense pact) may or may not result in military assistance if/when a post-Soviet state is under attack, especially when the attacker has an effective deterrent, such as nuclear arms deliverable against U.S. targets.

- U.S. intelligence and military assistance shortcomings are obvious. U.S. intelligence-gathering and analysis regarding the Russian threat to Georgia failed. The U.S. military assistance to Georgia, worth around $2 billion over the last 15 years and focused on the development of counterinsurgency capabilities instead of conventional warfare, did not prevent the August 2008 debacle. No scenarios of a Russian invasion were envisaged, wargamed, or seriously exercised. No force structure to resist a Russian invasion was built by the Georgian authorities with U.S. support. U.S. intelligence managers justified the failure by complaining that the satellite capabilities were redeployed for Iraq.[126] Other intelligence sources told the principal author that ample warning was provided to the George W. Bush administration.[127] Additionally, the war demonstrates that there is no substitute for high-quality human intelligence and raises questions with regards to the reporting chain to the National Security Command Authority.

- Air power is not sufficient. Russia used air, armor, the Black Sea Fleet, Special Forces, and allied militias in the attack. Clausewitzian lessons still apply to the August 2008 war: the use of overwhelming force against the enemy's center of gravity by implementing a combined air-land-sea operation may be 20th-century style, but it does work.[128]

- Surprise and speed of operations matter, as they have for the 4,000 years of recorded history of warfare. To be successful, wars must have limited and achievable goals. Russia achieved most of its goals between Friday and Monday, while the world, including President Bush, was watching the Olympics and parliaments were on vacation.

- Russia is prepared to take military casualties— within reason—and inflict overwhelming military and civilian casualties at a level unacceptable to the enemy. Georgia lost some 100-200 soldiers and effectively capitulated. A tougher enemy could well suffer a proportionally higher rate of casualties and keep on fighting.
- Information and psychological warfare is important. So is cyber security. It looks like during the war, the Russians conducted repeated denial-of-service attacks against Georgia (and in 2007, against Estonia), shutting down key websites. Russia was ready with accusations and footage of alleged Georgian atrocities in South Ossetia, shifting the information operation playing field to describing Georgia as an aggressor; portraying itself and its Ossetian allies as victims; saving Ossetian civilians from barbaric Georgians. These operations matter domestically, to shore up support and boost morale at home and to isolate the adversary and undermine his reputation internationally.
- International organizations failed to prevent the war and force Russia to observe the ceasefire conditions. This was because (1) Russia was classified as a "peacekeeper"—through a CIS-based mechanism before the war, in addition to effectively being a side in the conflict; and (2) Moscow enjoyed a veto power in two organizations that could play a peacekeeping role in Georgia: OSCE and the UN. Russia would not agree to a NATO peacekeeping force, while the EU expressed no sufficient interest in deploying a credible contingent in the Caucasus.

The Russia-Georgia war indicates that the balance of power in western Eurasia has shifted, and that U.S. power may be deteriorating in the face of its lengthy and open-ended commitments in Iraq, Afghanistan, Libya, and the Global War on Terror, which are leading to global overstretch. While the Middle East, and especially the Persian Gulf, will remain a top priority in U.S. foreign policy, Russia is playing an increasingly active role in the strategic environment along its southern tier, from the Black Sea to Afghanistan and western China.

THE RUSSIA-GEORGIA WAR AFTERMATH: REGIONAL IMPLICATIONS

The war demonstrated fissures in Europe between the Western powers eager to maintain good relations with Russia and the Eastern European states that, 20 years after the collapse of the USSR, retain a political memory of the Soviet occupation. Specifically, Germany, France, and Italy were anxious to put the war behind them and treated it as a nuisance, whereas the presidents of Poland, Ukraine, Estonia, and Lithuania and the Prime Minister of Latvia flew to Tbilisi during the war to stand shoulder to shoulder with Saakashvili.

The war also demonstrated weaknesses of NATO and the EU security system, since they provided no effective response to Russia's forcibly changing the borders and to the occupation of of an OSCE member state.

Washington Sending Mixed Signals

Vice President Joe Biden's trip to Ukraine and Georgia in the summer of 2009 failed to assuage fears that America may be abandoning its allies in the post-Soviet space. Instead, fudged messages and more confusion prevailed. The mere fact that the Vice President ventures into what Russia calls its "near abroad" 2 weeks after President Barack Obama's visit to Moscow raised concerns that the White House has downgraded its relationship with Ukraine and Georgia.

"Just as all states should have the right to choose their leaders, states must have the right to borders that are secure, and to their own foreign policies. That is true for Russia, just as it is true for the United States. . . . That's why we must apply this principle to all nations—and that includes nations like Georgia and Ukraine," declared President Obama in his June 7 Moscow speech. Yet, after Biden's visit, questions about Georgia's security remained unanswered.

The Obama administration believes that prioritizing the relationship with Moscow may address real needs in such vital areas as Afghanistan, Iran, and arms control. But while the global agenda is important, so is U.S credibility in Eurasia and among European allies.

Biden's trip to Georgia raised concerns, despite a hero's welcome there. Hundreds of Georgians lined the streets with slogans like, "Don't Forget Us" and "No to Occupation," in reference to Russia's presence on Georgian territory since the summer of 2008. Vice President Biden rebuffed Russia's claims to a 19thcentury-style sphere of influence. He delivered a message that the United States is seeking a free, secure, democratic, and united Georgia. But this declaration came with qualifications and was short on operational details.

Importantly, the Vice President rejected any physical security guarantees to Georgia in case of a Russian attack. Here, some creative ambiguity could be in order. Behind closed doors, Biden warned against any future use of force to liberate the Russian-occupied territories—a position inherited from the Clinton and Bush administrations—and rejected Georgia's requests for defensive weapons, such as anti-tank and anti-aircraft systems. More than a year later, this policy still prevails. The Obama administration is walking a tightrope between trying to improve the frayed relationship with Russia while simultaneously rejecting Moscow's spurious claims to a "sphere of privileged interests" in the former Soviet Union and Eastern and Central Europe.

To boost the confidence of U.S. allies, Washington should expand cooperation with NATO allies in formulating and implementing a joint policy that clearly delineates security "red lines" in Europe, including contingency planning for the defense of Eastern and Central European NATO members. Such planning, undertaken for the Baltic States after the Georgia war is a welcome beginning.

The United States should continue to cooperate with, upgrade, and improve the militaries in the post-Soviet states, especially Azerbaijan, Georgia, and Ukraine. It should work with post-Soviet states on developing democratic institutions, transparency, the rule of law, and good governance, since stronger institutions themselves enhance national security and improve the investment climate.

And to make clear American priorities in the region, the White House could announce a visit by President Obama to a non-Russian state in the region. The President could deliver a strong message of support for their sovereignty, territorial integrity, diplomatic and security cooperation, Euro–Atlantic integration, democratic development, and energy security. Eastern

Europe and Eurasia, the heart of the Eastern hemisphere, cannot and should not be neglected. Nor can they be abandoned to the geopolitical ambitions of those with transparent anti-American agendas. The U.S. Government should make certain that this message rings loud and clear.

IMPLICATION OF THE RUSSIA-GEORGIA WAR FOR IRANIAN CONTINGENCIES

In view of U.S. concerns with regard to the Iranian nuclear program, it is worth examining the repercussions of Russia's Georgian adventure on the control of the South Caucasus air space. We argue that Russia emboldened Iran by securing its northern tier through the denial of bases, airfields, electronic facilities, and other cooperation in Georgia and Azerbaijan to the United States, and possibly Israeli aerial operations.

Of course, growing tensions over Iran's nuclear program play an important role in Russia's policy in South Caucasus. In case of a hot conflict, Russia wants to be able to stop the deployment of U.S. military and allied forces in the Caucasus, including use of air bases. Russian control of South Caucasus air space from bases in Armenia and on Georgian territory in Abkhazia and South Ossetia will effectively deny U.S. air operations there without Moscow's consent.

At the same time, Russia is willing to strengthen Iranian air defenses. In 2007, Russia signed an agreement to supply Iran and secured its right to sell modern S-300 long-range anti-aircraft missiles to that country despite the third round of UN Security Council sanctions. The example of the Bushehr nuclear reactor, which Russia fueled in August 2010, demonstrates that Moscow fulfills prior agreements—albeit with delays.

The S-300 system, which has a radius of over 90 miles and effective altitudes of about 90,000 feet, is capable of tracking up to 100 targets simultaneously. It is considered one of the best in the world and is amazingly versatile—capable of shooting down aircraft, cruise missiles, and ballistic missile warheads.[5] The S-300 complements the Tor-M1 air defense missile system, also supplied by Russia. In 2007, Russia delivered 29 Tor-M1s worth $70 million to Iran.

The deployment of the anti-aircraft shield in Iran, if it occurs, effectively limits the window in which Israel or the United States could conduct an effective aerial campaign aimed at destroying, delaying, or crippling the Iranian nuclear program. The Islamic Republic will use the long-range anti-aircraft system, in addition to the point-defense TOR M-1 short-range Russian-made system, to protect its nuclear infrastructure, including suspected nuclear weapons facilities, from a potential U.S. or Israeli preventive strike.

BROADER REPERCUSSIONS OF THE WAR

Two years after the Russia-Georgia war, it is clear that the conflict changed the balance of power in post-Soviet Eurasia. Russia continues to strengthen its dominance in the region. It was reportedly involved in the April 2010 overthrow of Kyrgyzstan President Kurmanbek Bakyiev. It is pressuring Belarus to jettison strongman Alexander Lukashenka. In August

2010, Moscow tightened the screws on Georgia and Moldova by ordering its Customs Union partners, Kazakhstan and Belarus, to stop importing Georgian mineral water and Moldovan (and Georgian) wines.

Critics argue that the United States jettisoned 20 years of vigorous pursuit of a bipartisan engagement agenda in Eurasia. There was a lack of a robust U.S. response to these recent developments, stemming from the absence of a clear vision and policy for the region. On her recent visit to the Caucasus, Secretary of State Hillary Clinton mentioned the Russian occupation of Georgian territory. But she emphasized "soft power" over military challenges. Yet, Russia still speaks the language of arms. In the last 2 years it has built five military bases in Abkhazia and South Ossetia. In August 2010, Moscow also provided military guarantees to Armenia, assuming a joint responsibility with Yerevan to protect Armenia's borders against Azerbaijan and Turkey. This development shifts the balance of power in the region.

At the time of this writing, Prime Minister Vladimir Putin has prepared for President Medvedev's signature a draft protocol, which would not only commit forces on Russia's military base in Gyumri to share security responsibilities with the Armenian army, but also commit Russia to selling advanced weapons to the Armenians. Baku and Ankara expressed deep concern with these developments. According to the protocol, the Russians will remain in Gyumri until 2044, with an automatic 5-year lease extension. The previous contract called for the base to be dismantled in 2015. This arrangement is similar to that of the recently re-negotiated lease for the Sevastopol naval base, which is now extended to 2042.

The commitment of Russian forces to defend Armenia puts Azerbaijan in an untenable situation. Its efforts to reach out to Russia by selling gas and buying sophisticated weaponry so far has not borne fruit. It is a clear warning that, should Baku seek to regain the secessionist Nagorno-Karabakh as well as seven Armenian-occupied districts of Azerbaijan, it can expect to face Moscow's might. The subtext is clear as well: Azerbaijan should scale back cooperation with the West—or face the consequences.

Yet, Russia may sweeten this unsavory power pill. The respected *Vedomosti* newspaper reported that the Defense Ministry of Azerbaijan has contracted with Rosoboronexport to purchase two battalions' worth of the SA-20 Gargoyle (S-300PMU-2) Favorit anti-aircraft missile system. Russia's Defense Ministry subsequently denied the report, but the Azeri Defense Ministry did not.

In Eurasia, then, Moscow is using its entire toolbox to shift the balance of power in the region in its favor. Its tools include diplomacy (including recognition of the self-proclaimed republics), strategic information operations, arms sales, status-of-forces agreements, base construction—even regime change—to secure its sphere of privileged interests.

GEORGIA IN THE AFGHANISTAN SUPPLY CHAIN

The United States depends on Russian influence in Eurasia when considering the supply of the NATO forces deployed in Afghanistan. Alternative bypasses to the Russia-centered Northern Distribution Network (NDN) are thus of importance to U.S. strategists and logisticians. President Mikheil Saakashvili offered Georgia to become a logistical hub for NATO's operations in Afghanistan. This offer, unveiled in an interview to the Associated Press (AP), came only days after NATO finalized a supply-route agreement with Kazakhstan.

While a supply route through Georgia already functions (for equipment, not armaments), U.S. officials have not immediately accepted Saakashvili's new proposal. Washington may prefer to cooperate with Russia, giving it a stake in the Afghan engagement.

Saakashvili offered Georgia's Black Sea ports of Poti and Batumi for transshipping military supplies, and the country's airports for refueling cargo planes. The AP quoted Pentagon officials as saying that the U.S. Defense Department was aware of Saakashvili's offer, but had not explored the proposal. The late U.S. Special Representative for Afghanistan and Pakistan Ambassador Richard Holbrooke visited Georgia on February 21-22, 2010. He planned to meet Saakashvili and visit Georgian troops at the Krtsanisi National Training Center and observe their training for the operation in Afghanistan. Reportedly, the issue of Georgia as a supply route for the Afghan war was on the table.

Georgia has been utilized as a transit point for shipment of nonlethal cargos. "The route to Afghanistan is already used extensively, because almost 80 percent of cargo which is not going through the Pakistan route is going through Georgia and only 20 percent through Russia already," said Alexander Rondeli, President of the Georgian Foundation for Security in International Studies (GFSIS).[129]

Saakashvili's offer was not particularly remarkable, because the United States is covering all the bases by operating NDN via Russia and Kazakhstan, as well as its southern branch via Georgia and Azerbaijan across the Caspian Sea to Central Asia. Negotiations between the United States and the South Caucasus states for new supply routes have been underway since March 2009. The U.S. European Command held a conference in Baku on March 9 and 10, 2010, aimed at exploring possible supply routes through the region. Government officials from Azerbaijan, Georgia, and Turkey met with U.S military representatives to discuss transit possibilities.

NATO and Kazakhstan signed an agreement on January 27, 2010, that permits NATO allies to ship cargo bound for Afghanistan through Kazakh territory. The agreement completed the northern supply route, which allows overland passage of cargo from Europe to Afghanistan.

The agreement with Kazakhstan, unlike Saakashvili's recent proposal, allows NATO allies to ship only nonlethal cargo through Kazakh territory by rail. It will then pass on to Uzbekistan before reaching its final destination.

In 2009, the U.S. Defense Department said the U.S. transportation command sent 75 percent of supplies for the war through Pakistan. An agreement with Russia, signed in summer 2009, allows NATO flights with troops and weapons through the Russian airspace. The passage of some flights, however, became hampered by bureaucracy.

NATO's second alternative to Pakistan involves Georgia and Central Asia. Supplies coming by ship can dock at ports in the Mediterranean (Turkey) and the Black Sea (Russia or Georgia), and from there could cross via Kazakhstan and Uzbekistan and into northern Afghanistan. Another possibility for goods arriving in Georgia or Turkey would be a route through Azerbaijan, across the Caspian Sea, Turkmenistan, and then into northwest Afghanistan.

In January 2009, General David Petraeus, then-commander of the U.S. Central Command, said that deals for supply routes to Afghanistan have been reached with Russia and several Central Asian countries. At that time General Petraeus did not provide any specifics.

As opposed to the Pakistani option and the northern route through Russia, the route originating in Georgia would be the shortest. The only potential drawback of the route is the possibility of a terrorist attack on the supply lines. The Georgian security services are aware that such a route is a high priority target for radical Islamists. But geopolitical concerns might hamper U.S. officials from striking a deal with Georgia, analysts say. "Russia is a big problem here; no one wants to irritate that," Rondeli said.[130]

Personalities of the countries' leaders might also be in their way. Russia would remain irritated with Saakashvili, no matter what. Russia, being an integral part of the Northern Distribution Route, could also be in competition with Georgia over providing logistical support to NATO. Russia, of course, has a stake in a secure Afghanistan.

However, analysts agree that Georgia's motivation in providing supply routes for NATO armaments is to illustrate that Tbilisi is interested not only in consuming security, but in contributing to it. The supply route is important for the defeat of such radical Islamist movements in Afghanistan as al Qaeda and the Taliban. Therefore, Georgia is participating together with other countries in a joint operation to defeat the enemies of the West.

RUSSIAN TROOP MOVEMENTS AND ACTIVITY IN GEORGIA: FOMENTING POLITICAL UNREST

During the spring of 2009, the Russian Federation significantly increased its military presence in the occupied Georgian territories of Abkhazia and South Ossetia. An intensified military buildup took place, particularly in the territories adjacent to the separation lines in Abkhazia and the Tskhinvali region. In parallel with this buildup, there has been increased maneuvering of Russia's Black Sea Fleet close to the waters around Abkhazia and regular patrolling of Georgian airspace over Abkhazia. These latter actions were conducted in the wake of the April 9 opposition rallies in Georgia, adding tension to an already complicated situation.

On April 10, the Georgian Ministry of Defense accused Russia of reinforcing its military presence in the breakaway regions of Abkhazia and South Ossetia.[131] Contemporaneously, Foreign Minister Grigol Vashadze announced that he is "highly concerned" about a buildup of Russian troops and heavy infantry on the two regions' administrative borders with Georgian-controlled territory.[132]

It is possible that Russia was trying to send a signal of support to the anti-Saakashvili forces. Russian troops were reported to be gathering in the Akhalgori region of Georgia—a mere 25 miles from Tbilisi. In an April 8 statement to reporters, Deputy Interior Minister Eka Zghuladze said that 150 Russian armored vehicles had been moved to Akhalgori in South Ossetia, and 35 such vehicles entered the district of Gali in southern Abkhazia. Russian planes have been patrolling both regions since April 7 (the SU-25s over-flights in South Ossetia and over Abkhazia). According to a Georgian official, Russian troops are also on high alert.[133] This includes the whole 58th Army in the North Caucasus military district.

President Saakashvili stated in an interview on April 11 that Russia has 5,000 troops stationed in each of the breakaway regions. Saakashvili also went on to say that that despite the large-scale military buildup of the Russian forces both in the breakaway regions and on Georgia's borders, he did not think that Russia would "renew any large-scale military adventure."[134] Instead, he declared that these movements are aimed at "possible internal unrests [in Georgia]."[135]

Large-scale protests planned by Georgian opposition leaders to unseat Saakashvili began in the spring of 2009. The number of protestors had declined sharply from 60,000 on its first day to roughly 2,000 by the 7th day.[136] In fact, they had taken a time-out until Tuesday for Georgian Easter. Saakashvili called for direct dialogue with the opposition. However, though Irakli Alasania, leader of the Alliance for Georgia coalition, stated that he is ready for dialogue, other opposition leaders are against it.

The so-called "radical opposition," which includes former Parliamentary Speaker Nino Burjanadze and former Foreign Minister Salome Zourabishvili, has flatly refused any offer for dialogue short of Saakashvili's resignation.[137] Saakashvili has suggested that Russian money has figured into the protests.[138] When asked about sponsors of the opposition, Saakashvili stated: "Most of the money—millions of dollars— comes from Russian oligarchs. I have documentary proof of that, which I am not making public yet. Whether the money is being sent from Russia under the supervision of the Russian government, that I do not know."[139] In addition to internal intervention, Russia is beefing up military capabilities, specifically naval assets, which make Georgia and other neighbors, such as Baltic States, nervous.

LESSONS FROM THE WAR'S NAVAL OPERATIONS: THE *MISTRAL* ASSAULT SHIP SALE

Russian military leaders pointed out the slow pace of naval and ship-to-shore deployments in the Georgian war and suggested a radical way to address the drawback. As noted, Russia wants to buy the French *Mistral* assault ships. In early 2010, French President Nicolas Sarkozy approved plans to sell such a ship to Russia. If it occurs, it would be the first major Russian warship purchased from the West since World War I—and it may indicate a modernization breakthrough for Russian military procurement. However, NATO, of which France is a member, does not seem concerned. Secretary-General Anders Fogh Rasmussen announced through a spokesman that the Alliance does not consider Russia a threat to NATO or any allied nation. Baltic nations and Georgia beg to differ.

As Russia is not yet a trusted partner to NATO, the United States and NATO could object to such a sale, as it imperils the security of the Alliance's members and aspirants. France is trying to benefit from naval sales while ignoring concerns of NATO members and allies, such as Georgia and the three Baltic states.

As its Soviet-era industrial base deteriorates, the Russian leadership apparently has given up on its indigenous naval-building capacities. Turning away from the Soviet-era autarky, Moscow is planning to buy sophisticated armaments, such as *Mistral*s or Israeli UAVs, then reverse-engineer them or produce them under license, to force-march its obsolescent military through the 21st century.

In a new appropriations and acquisition policy, and in a break from past practices when all military systems were built at home, Moscow wants to "buy one, build three" *Mistral*s under the French license. At 23,700 tons and 210 meters long, the ship will be smaller only than aircraft carriers. And it has leading-edge command, control, communications, and intelligence capabilities.

The ship, carrying up to two landing barges, 30 helicopters, 900 commandos, 13 tanks, and numerous armored vehicles, will be a formidable power projection tool. Russian ship-based attack helicopters are particularly important for naval reach and punch. Vladimir Putin has made no secret that he would deploy the *Mistral*-class ships wherever he wants.

Taking history into account, Russian naval modernization should make NATO worry. Since the 18th century, Russia has traditionally built up its smaller sea fleets in the Baltic and the Black Sea before upgrading to the blue-water navies. Europe's acquiescence in the face of the Russian power projection aspirations is both obvious and disturbing.

First, Russia snubbed President Nicolas Sarkozy when it refused to comply with the Georgia war ceasefire agreement he signed with President Medvedev in August 2008. Second, Russia recently conducted a military exercise against Poland, using a 900-strong tank attack force. NATO did not protest. Third, Russia changed laws, allowing it to deploy troops abroad by presidential fiat only, without any parliamentary approval. Finally, President Medvedev recently signed a new military doctrine, which allows Russia to protect vaguely defined "compatriots" and to lower the threshold for preemptive nuclear strikes.

NATO, meanwhile, proceeded to build bridges with Russia. This is understandable, since the supply route to Afghanistan is vital—and it passes through Russia and its allies in Central Asia. The U.S. Government was mum on announcements regarding *Mistral* sales as well. Washington wanted to complete the negotiations of the Strategic Arms Reduction Talks follow-on treaty. It also expected Moscow to throw a lifeline to the U.S.-Iran policy by supporting the sanctions on Iran at the UN Security Council in order to entice the ayatollahs to stop their nuclear program. Russia supported the sanctions, but Teheran did not budge on its nuclear program's transparency. Washington also does not want to antagonize the Elysee, as President Obama hopes Sarkozy will send more French troops to Afghanistan.

However, the *Mistral* security threat is significant. Instead of advising Paris to postpone the sale indefinitely in view of Russia's threatening posture toward Georgia, the U.S. position is not to oppose the sale of *Mistral*, while opposing the sales of advanced electronic and weapons system on board the ship. Plans may change in the future, but today the *Mistral* sale would be sending a wrong signal to NATO allies, to NATO aspirants, and to the Russians.

At a time when Moscow still views NATO as an adversary, abandons the Conventional Forces in Europe Treaty, and occupies 20 percent of Georgian territory, a major warship sale to the Russian Navy is premature. This is especially true when the sale is a part of a major naval modernization, which may jeopardize NATO's flanks and important energy routes. NATO members should expand military cooperation with Russia only after it fulfills the August 2008 Medvedev-Sarkozy ceasefire agreement and restores its credibility and friendship with the West.

Russian Deployment of S-300 Missiles in the Caucasus

In August 2010, General Alexander Zelin, the commander of the Russian air force, announced that Moscow had deployed a state-of-the-art S-300 (SA-20 Favorit) long range air defense system in Abkhazia. According to Zelin, the task of the air defense systems is "to prevent violation of Abkhaz and South Ossetian airspace and to destroy any aircraft intruding into their airspace no matter what their purpose might be."[140] However, there is much more than defense of Abkhazia to the Russian deployment. Taken together with the air force deployment and S-300 base in Armenia, that brings the strategic air space over South Caucasus and parts of the Black Sea under further Russian control.

P. J. Crowley, former U.S. Assistant Secretary of State and State Department spokesman, said: "I believe it's our understanding that Russia has had S-300 missiles in Abkhazia for the past 2 years." He later claimed that this is "not necessarily" a new development.[141] However, with this move, Russia is yet again violating the August 2008 ceasefire agreement, negotiated by the French President Nicolas Sarkozy. It called upon both countries to withdraw troops to prewar positions and restore the *status quo ante bellum*. Instead, Russia has built at least five military bases in Abkhazia and South Ossetia in the past 2 years alone.

Although the range of the system is about 120 miles, the deployment has to be seen in the context of recent Russian policies in the Caucasus, particularly Moscow's recently negotiated extention of a contract for basing troops in the Armenian Gyumri military base till 2042. It will assume joint control over Armenian borders. As the leading member of CSTO, Russia controls air space over Armenia. Now Moscow is reportedly considering a sale of an S-300 air defense system to Azerbaijan.

There is a clear strategy behind these actions. While Secretary of State Clinton hails "soft power" in the Caucasus, Moscow engages in a hard, classic political-military power projection in this strategic region, which connects the Atlantic (via the Black Sea and Mediterranean) with the energy riches of Eurasia. As President Medvedev stated in his oft-mentioned postwar 2008 speech, this is "a zone of Russian privileged interests," where it is willing to use force.[142]

Most importantly from the U.S. perspective, Russian actions are aimed at denying the United States airspace and over-flight options. The surveillance aspect is no less important— depending on the actual deployment of the air defenses, with the associated radars able to picture or "paint" much of western Georgia and the adjoining Black Sea coastline. The ultimate objective for Moscow is to become an uncontested hegemon in the South Caucasus. Of course, this has potential implications in case of an Iranian contingency.

The Russians are committed to deployments in the Caucasus that lead to the strategic denial of U.S. power projection in that region. This bears on America's future ability to resupply Afghanistan, use power to disarm a nuclear Iran, ensure the energy supply from the Caspian, and help pro-Western friends and allies.

CONCLUSION

The Russian leadership focused on Georgia as the key element in its strategy to reassert its power in Eurasia. For years before the 2008 invasion, Moscow sought a pretext for a war that would provide a payback for the NATO operation solidifying Kosovo independence, reestablish Russian domination in Abkhazia and South Ossetia, and demonstrate the consequences of NATO aspirations for a post-Soviet state.

Taken together, this was "the privileged sphere of interests" in action, 21st-century style.[143]

In Eurasia, Moscow is using its entire toolbox to shift the balance of power in the region. Its tools include diplomacy (e.g., recognition of the self-proclaimed republics), strategic information operations, arms sales, status-of-forces agreements, and base construction—even regime change—to secure its control over the "sphere of privileged interests." The 2008 Georgia war was an important step toward the realization of this goal.

End Notes

[1] Temur Yakobashvili, Deputy Prime Minister and Minister of Reintegration of Georgia, personal interview, May 23, 2010.

[2] Georgian armed forces and Ministry of Defense officials, names withheld by request, interview with secondary author, December 2008.

[3] Svante Cornell and S. Frederick Starr, eds., *The Guns of August 2008: Russia's War in Georgia*, London, UK: M. E. Sharpe, 2009, p. 166.

[4] Felix K. Chang, "Russia Resurgent: An Initial Look at Russian Military Performance in Georgia," Foreign Policy Research Institute, August 13, 2008, p. 2.

[5] Cornell and Starr, eds., pp. 171-173.

[6] Ronald D. Asmus, *A Little War That Shook the World*, New York: Palgrave-MacMillan, 2010, p. 165.

[7] Alexander Nicolle, ed., "Russia's Rapid Reaction: But Short War Shows Lack of Modern Systems," *IISS Strategic Comments*, Vol. 14, Issue 7, September 2008, p. 2.

[8] Asmus, p. 180.

[9] Tor Bukvoll, "Russia's Military Performance in Georgia," *Military Review*, November-December 2009, p. 59.

[10] Mikhail Barabanov, Lavrov Anton, Viacheslav Tseluyko, Moscow, Russia: *Tanki Avgusta* (*Tanks of August*), Tsentr analiza strategii i technologii (Center for Analysis of Strategies and Technologies), 2009, p. 46.

[11] The preceding three sentences are taken from Robert E. Hamilton, "After August: Causes, Results and Policy Implications of the Russo-Georgian War," U.S. Army War College Strategic Research Project, Carlisle, PA, 2009.

[12] Asmus, p. 30.

[13] Baltic intelligence official, interview with primary author, March 2008.

[14] C. W. Blandy, "Provocation, Deception, Entrapment: The Russo-Georgia Five Day War," *Advanced Research and Assessment Group Caucasus Series* Issue 09/01, Shrivenham, UK: Defence Academy of the United Kingdom, p. 2.

[15] Asmus, p. 166.

[16] Interview, senior official of the Bush Administration who requested anonymity, October 2009, Washington, DC.

[17] Blandy, p. 4.

[18] Asmus, p. 20.

[19] *Ibid.*, p. 20.

[20] Cornell and Starr, eds., p. 151.

[21] *Ibid.*, p. 150.

[22] *Ibid.*, p. 153.

[23] For an overview and analysis of Georgian planning and operations, see Robert E. Hamilton, "The Bear Came Through the Tunnel: An Analysis of Georgian Planning and Operation in the Russo-Georgian War and Implications for U.S. Policy," *Crisis in the Caucasus: Russia, Georgia and the West*, Oxon, UK: Routledge, 2010, pp. 202-234.

[24] Roger N. McDermott, "Russia's Conventional Armed Forces and the Georgia War," *Parameters*, Spring 2009, p. 70.

[25] Mikhail Barabanov, "The August War Between Russia and Georgia," *Moscow Defense Brief #3*, 2008, p. 10.

[26] Official Georgian Government Timeline, released August 21, 2008, p. 14.

[27] *Ibid.*, p. 10.

[28] Bukvoll, p. 57.

[29] *Ibid.*, p. 58.

[30] *Ibid.*, p. 58.

[31] Asymmetric Warfare Group, "Russian-Republic of Georgia Conflict," *Joint Center for Operational Analysis Journal*, Spring 2009, p. 9.

[32] *Ibid.,* p. 11.

[33] Bukvoll, p. 59.

[34] Asymmetric Warfare Group, p. 11.

[35] Georgian armed forces and Ministry of Defense officials, names withheld by request, interview with secondary author, December 2008.

[36] *Ibid.,* p. 58.

[37] Margarete Klein, "Military Implications of the Georgia War: Russian Armed Forces in Need of Reform," *The Caucasus Crisis: International Perceptions and Policy Implications for Germany and Europe,* Berlin, Germany: German Institute for International and Security Affairs, November, 2008, p. 13.

[38] Cornell and Starr, eds., p. 166.

[39] *Ibid.,* p. 166.

[40] Klein, p. 14.

[41] Paul Rich, ed., *Crisis in the Caucasus: Russia, Georgia and the West*, Oxon, UK: Routledge, 2010, p. 160.

[42] Senior Georgian official who requested anonymity, interview with primary author, May 23, 2010. This assertion is unconfirmed and might be contradicted by the official Georgian government timeline of the conflict, which lists three Georgian tanks destroyed by South Ossetian militia on the first day of the war (although it does not name the weapons system that destroyed them).

[43] Rich, ed., p. 160.

[44] Cornell and Starr, eds., p. 167.

[45] Senior Georgian official who requested anonymity, interview with primary author, May 23, 2010.

[46] Rich, ed., p. 161.

[47] Klein, p. 14.

[48] Rich, ed., p. 157.

[49] *Ibid.,* p. 157.

[50] Bukvoll, p. 58.

[51] Nicoll, ed., p. 2.

[52] McDermott, p. 66.

[53] Bukvoll, p. 58.

[54] Rich, ed., p. 159. Carolina Vendil Pallin and Frederik Westerlund say that Russian use of PGMs might have been limited by the low clouds that blanketed the theater during much of the war. This would have restricted the use of laser- and television-guided weapons, which make up the bulk of the Russian PGM inventory.

[55] Rich, ed., p. 159.

[56] Bukvoll, p. 59.

[57] Rich, ed., p. 158.

[58] Cornell and Starr, eds., p. 167.

[59] Colonel Matt Brand, U.S. Defense and Army Attache to Georgia, interview with secondary author, September 11, 2008.

[60] Bukvoll, p. 59.

[61] Cornell and Starr, eds., p. 168.

[62] *Ibid.,* p. 168.

[63] Chang, p. 2.

[64] Rich, ed., p. 160.

[65] Bukvoll, p. 58.

[66] Georgian Government Document, DTG.

[67] Barabanov, Anton, and Tseluyko, p. 76.

[68] Asymmetric Warfare Group, p. 13.

[69] Major Giorgi Kalandadze, Commander, 4th Georgian Infantry Brigade, interview with secondary author, December 2008.

[70] Asymmetric Warfare Group, p. 12.

[71] Interview with secondary author, June 15, 2010.

[72] Bukvoll, p. 59.

[73] Asmus, p. 167.

[74] David Bertold's son, interview, August 2008.

[75] Cornell and Starr, eds., p. 191.

[76] *Ibid.,* p. 183.

[77] Rich, ed., p. 154.

[78] *Ibid.,* p. 3.

[79] Asymmetric Warfare Group, p. 12.

[80] Cornell and Starr, eds., p. 154.

[81] *Ibid.,* p. 188.

[82] *Ibid.*

[83] McDermott, p. 68.

[84] *Ibid.*

[85] Barabanov, Anton, and Tseluyko, p. 7.

[86] Interview with Advisor to the Minister of Defense, Moscow, September 8, 2009. The source requested anonymity.

[87] McDermott, p. 69.

88 Nicoll, ed., p. 2.

[89] Cornell and Starr, eds., p. 167.

[90] McDermott, p. 70.

[91] *Ibid.,* p. 71.

[92] Cornell and Starr, eds., pp. 3, 149.

[93] Barabanov, Anton, and Tseluyko, pp. 106-107.

[94] McDermott, p. 77.

[95] Pavel Felgenhauer, "Rearmament Declared the Main Issue in Russian Military Reform," *Eurasia Daily Monitor,* Vol. 7, Issue 122, June 24, 2010, p. 1.

[96] McDermott, p. 75.

[97] Felgenhauer, p. 1.

[98] *Ibid.*

[99] Dmitri Gorenburg, "Medvedev's Military Priorities for 2010," available from *russiamil.wordpress.com/2009/11/18/ medvedevs-military-priorities-for-2010/.*

[100] Felgenhauer, p. 2.

[101] Owen Matthews, "The New Red Army," November 20, 2009, p. 3, available from *newsweek.com.*

[102] Bukvoll, p. 60.

[103] "Russia, Israel Sign Military Cooperation Agreement," September 12, 2010, available from *www.rferl.org/content/Russia Israel_Sign_Military_Cooperation_Agreement/2150123.html* .

[104] Felgenhauer, p. 2.

[105] *Ibid.,* p. 2.

[106] *Ibid.*

[107] Klein, p. 15.

[108] *Ibid.,* p. 16.

[109] *Ibid.*

[110] Bukvoll, p. 61.

[111] Name withheld by request, interview with primary author, June 15, 2010. This official claims that the pilfered share of the procurement budget is 50-60 percent.

[112] Keir Giles, "The Military Doctrine of the Russian Federation 2010," *Research Review,* Rome, Italy: NATO Defense Colllege, February, 2010, p. 1.

[113] *Ibid.*

[114] *Ibid.,* p. 5.

[115] *Ibid.,* p. 7.

[116] For information on Russian probes of foreign airspace, see David Blair, "RAF Jets Intercept Eight Russian Bombers," *The Telegraph* (UK), September 7, 2007; Matthew Hickley, "RAF Jets Scrambled as Russian Bombers Join War Manoeuvres off Atlantic Coast," *The Daily Mail Online,* January 22, 2008; and "Russian Bombers Probe Canadian Airspace," *Grog News,* July 30, 2010.

[117] Senior Russian official, interview with primary author, June 15, 2010.

[118] Giles, p. 2.

[119] *Ibid.,* p. 3.

[120] *Ibid.,* p. 8.

[121] Bukvoll, p. 58.

[122] Rich, ed., p. 163.

[123] Giles, p. 8.

[124] Dr. Stephen Blank, interview with primary author, Washington, DC, May 2010.

[125] *Asmus, p. 7.*

[126] *Ibid.*, p. 2.

[127] Personal interview with then-U.S. senior intelligence official who requested anonymity.

[128] Martin Sieff, "Defense Focus: Underestimating Russia. Russian Army Shocks West in Georgia Ops," United Press International 20080812-002422-8913, August 12, 2008.

[129] Press Release, Remarks by President Obama at the New Economic School Graduation, July 7, 2009, available from *www. whitehouse.gov/the_press_office/Remarks-By-The-President-At-TheNew-Economic-School-Graduation.*

[130] Lizaveta Zhahanina, "Georgia-US Discussing Supply Route to Afghanistan," *The Georgian Times*, March 22, 2010, available from *www.geotimes.ge/index.php?m=home&newsid=20515.*

[131] *Ibid.*

[132] "Georgia: Tbilisi Suspects Russia of Military Build-Up," *EurasiaNet*, April 10, 2009, available from *www.eurasianet.org/ departments/news/articles/eav041009a.shtml.*

[133] "Georgia's Anti-Saakashvili Protests Enter Third Day," *Radio Free Europe*, April 11, 2009, available from *www.rferl.org/ content/Georgias_AntiSaakashvili_Protests_Enter_Third_ Day/1606862.html.*

[134] "Saakashvili Sees No Threat of Russia's 'New Military Adventurer'," *Civil Georgia*, April 14, 2009, available from *www. civil.ge/eng/article.php?id=20727;* Isabel Gorst, "Moscow Urges NATO to Cancel Georgia Exercises," *Georgian Daily*, April 16, 2009, available from *georgiandaily.com/index.php?option=com_cont ent&task=view&id=11140&Itemid=65.*

[135] "Saakashvili Sees No Threat of Russia's 'New Military Adventurer'," *Civil Georgia*, April 14, 2009, available from *www. civil.ge/eng/article.php?id=20727.*

[136] "Numbers Dwindle in Georgia Protests," *Georgian Daily*, April 15, 2009, available from *georgiandaily.com/index. php?option=com_content&task=view&id=11123&Itemid=133.*

[137] Molly Corso, "Opposition Ready for Dialogue on Its Terms," *Eurasianet*, April 16, 2009, available from *www.eurasianet. org/departments/insightb/articles/eav041609d.shtml.*

[138] Margarita Antidze and Matt Robinson, "Georgia Resists Moscow-inspired unrest: Saakashvili," *Reuters*, April 14, 2009, available from *www.reuters.com/article/worldNews/id USTRE53D2NN20090414.*

[139] "Saakashvili: Russian Oligarchs Fund Georgian Opposition," *Civil Georgia*, April 12, 2009, available from *www.civil.ge/ eng/article.php?id=20717.*

[140] "Russia Deploys S-300 Missiles in Abkhazia," *The Georgian Times*, August 11, 2010, available from *www.geotimes.ge/index. php?m=home&newsid=22527.*

[141] *Ibid.*

[142] BBC News, "Russia 'deploys missiles' in breakaway region of Abkhazia," August 11, 2010, available from *www.bbc.co.uk/ news/world-asia-pacific-10940297.*

[143] Remarks by President Medvedev during an interview with members of the Russian media, August 31, 2009, available from *medvedev-da.ru/about/news/index.php?ELEMENT_ID=4390.*

INDEX